Teaching
Class
Clowns

(And What They Can Teach Us)

William Watson Purkey
Foreword by Sally Butzin

CORWIN PRESS
A SAGE Publications Company
Thousand Oaks, California

A PRAYER FOR CLOWNS

God bless all clowns
Who star the world with laughter
Who ring the rafters
With a flying jest,
Who make the world spin merry on its way
And somehow add more beauty to each day.
God bless all clowns
So poor the world would be
Lacking their piquant touch, hilarity,
The belly-laughs, the ringing, lovely mirth
That makes a friendly place on this earth
God bless all clowns
Give them a long good life,
Make bright their way—they're a race apart!
All comest most who turn their hearts' pain
Into a dazzling jest to lift the heart
God bless all clowns.

—Poem read by Dick Van Dyke at Stan Laurel's funeral. Author of poem unknown; quoted in *Mr. Laurel and Mr. Hardy: An Affectionate Biography* by John McCabe, Garden City, NY: Doubleday, 1961/1985.

*This book is dedicated to
seven future leaders, scholars,
and perhaps one or two class
clowns—my wonderful grandchildren:*

*Jason Gaines, Natalie Gaines,
Jimmy Norton, Emily Norton,
Rebecca Purkey, Winston Purkey,
and one great grandson,
Dylan Dyer, the miracle baby.*

For information:

Corwin Press
A Sage Publications Company
2455 Teller Road
Thousand Oaks, California 91320
E-mail: order@corwinpress.com

Sage Publications Ltd.
1 Oliver's Yard
55 City Road
London EC1Y 1SP
United Kingdom

Sage Publications India Pvt. Ltd.
B-42, Panchsheel Enclave
Post Box 4109
New Delhi 110 017 India

Printed in the United States of America.

Library of Congress Cataloging-in-Publication Data

Purkey, William Watson.
Teaching class clowns (and what they can teach us) / by William Watson Purkey.
     p. cm.
Includes bibliographical references and index.
ISBN 1-4129-3724-8 (cloth) — ISBN 1-4129-3725-6 (pbk.)
     1. Classroom management. 2. Teacher-student relationships. 3. Comedians.
4. Joking. I. Title.
LB3013.P874 2006
371.102′4—dc22

                                                          2005032723

This book is printed on acid-free paper.

Graphic Artist: Dan Calabrese

06   07   08   09   10   11   9   8   7   6   5   4   3   2   1

Acquisitions Editor:	Faye Zucker
Editorial Assistant:	Gem Rabanera
Project Editor:	Tracy Alpern
Copy Editor:	Cheryl Duksta
Proofreader:	Ellen Brink
Typesetter:	C&M Digitals (P) Ltd.
Indexer:	Kirsten Kite
Cover Designer:	Lisa Miller

Contents

Foreword

*T*eaching Class Clowns (And What They Can Teach Us) is a joy to read. I laughed out loud as each chapter unfolded. Dr. Purkey recounts many humorous stories from his personal escapades as a former class clown and those of class clowns he has known.

The book is very well researched, with numerous examples of the famous and not-so-famous who morphed from class clowns into successful entertainers and leaders. There are many poignant quotes from these folks, commenting on their own painful classroom memories of the teachers who disparaged their talents. There are also hopeful and helpful stories of the teachers who laughed along and encouraged them to use their talents productively.

The author also provides the specific characteristics of class clowns that we all could emulate to become more positive and fulfilled as individuals. He further offers specific strategies that teachers can use to channel the class clown's energy and wisecracks into constructive classroom synergy.

Teaching Class Clowns is a gem. I highly recommend it to educators and parents, as well as anyone who enjoys a good laugh.

—Sally Butzin
Author, *Joyful Classrooms in an Age of Accountability*
Executive Director, Institute for School Innovation

Preface

As this book is written, the world finds itself in "another fine mess," as the portly Mr. Oliver Hardy of *Laurel & Hardy* fame would say. Newspapers are filled with grim news. Television, radio, magazines, the Internet, and other media remind us regularly of American military and civilian causalities, orange alerts, terrorism plots, deadly hurricanes, worldwide warming, massive national debt, natural catastrophes, and the proliferation of nuclear and other weapons of mass destruction. There is little room left for joy.

Schools in particular are becoming humorless places of high-stakes testing, ruthless competition, mandatory grade retention, and potential or real violence. Students are becoming nervous, depressed, angry, and aggressive. Teachers are feeling overburdened with the demand to "leave no child behind," while striving to meet requirements for higher student performance on standardized tests.

In her 2005 book *Joyful Classrooms*, Sally (Sarah) Butzin points out that mandatory retention of students is a constant threat. It hangs over each child's head like the sword of Damocles, hanging from the ceiling by a single hair. Butzin reports that we now have some children facing their third year in a grade because they could not pass one or more tests.

Heavy emphasis on high-stakes testing has resulted in a narrow curriculum. Teachers are forced to "teach to the test." A growing number of schools have been placed on "watch lists" or labeled as "at risk" or "failing" by local, state, and federal agencies. Adding to the threat of academic failure, schools are terrified over the possibility of being labeled by the No Child Left Behind legislation as "persistently dangerous," the scarlet letter of the education community. Most educators would rather have their school labeled "academically failing" than "persistently dangerous."

Average classroom teachers, who are already overburdened, are expected to teach at-risk and mainstreamed children, raise standards, show AYP (annual yearly progress), and at the same time prevent students from dropping out. Perhaps never before in American education has there been a more pervasive feeling of unhappiness and gloom. More good teachers are leaving the teaching profession because of joyless conditions. There is a great need for laughter, fun, and cheerfulness in classrooms and schools.

An overlooked gold mine of classroom humor and fun may be found in the contributions of class clowns. These impresarios of classroom entertainment have been almost totally neglected in the professional education literature. Hundreds of books, if not thousands, have been written about gifted and talented students. A similar number have been written about children with special needs. Yet almost nothing has been written on how to understand class clowns and appreciate their contributions. The same is true when it comes to teaching class clowns.

The neglect of class clowns is also apparent in books on humor written for larger audiences. In the comprehensive reference book *Encyclopedia of 20th-Century American Humor* (Nilsen & Nilsen), published in 2002, there is not a single reference to class clowns. The same is true of the *Random House Webster's Wit and Humor*

Quotationary (Frank), published in 2000. It is time to correct this situation by giving class clowns the recognition and appreciation they deserve.

Class clowns help meet the need for cheerfulness through their energy, sense of humor, and playful spirit. They encourage us to laugh more and live longer. They inspirit us with their love of life. Class clowns invite us to take a more lighthearted approach to living.

A middle school teacher provided an example of how a class clown can brighten a classroom. She was being observed by the principal (another state mandate), and, to impress the principal with her pedagogical skills, the teacher demonstrated a math process and then asked, "Does anyone know why I performed this function?" The resident class clown instantly responded, "Yeah. It's because the principal's sitting there." Later, the teacher and principal had a big laugh over the clown's response.

This book identifies four signature tendencies of class clowns. These tendencies are similar to Martin Seligman's signature strengths, described in his 2002 book *Authentic Happiness.* Signature tendencies are special characteristics that class clowns value and seek to practice every day. These tendencies provide valuable clues as to how teachers can be successful in understanding, appreciating, and teaching class clowns. Equally important, this book describes what class clowns can teach us about living a more cheerful life, personally and professionally.

Information presented in *Teaching Class Clowns* is gained from three primary sources. The first source is my own experience as a class clown. I can never remember a time when I was not hooked on humor. By the time I was sixty months old, I was totally committed to clowning.

The second source is a large-scale research study of class clowns conducted at the University of Florida. Dr. Sandra Damico and I studied 96 class clowns identified from a population of 3,500 eighth-grade public school students. Details of our research appeared in *The American Educational Research Journal* (Damico & Purkey, 1979).

The third source is my review of the life history of professional comedians, both classic and contemporary. In virtually every case, professional comedians began their careers as class clowns. According to Steve Allen, author of *The Funny Men,* if you are not a class clown by the time you are twelve years old, don't even think about becoming a professional comedian.

This book is not designed to help people become class clowns. Rather, *Teaching Class Clowns* provides teachers and others with an understanding and appreciation of a very special and talented group of students. It identifies effective ways to teach class clowns.

Equally important, this book suggests what class clowns can teach us. My hope is that *Teaching Class Clowns* will invite a more joyful, optimistic, fun-filled, humane, and caring environment for everyone in and around schools.

Acknowledgments

There is a special group of friends, colleagues, and class clowns I want to thank for their valuable suggestions for *Teaching Class Clowns:* Toody Byrd, Sally Butzin, Rebekah Carpenter, Zach Clements, Claudia Cornett, William Cosh, Tim Cusak, Patrick Davis, Richard and Carol Hedrick, Judy Lehr, Jane Mitchell, John Novak, Anne and Fred Richards, Don Russell, Jack Schmidt, Tom Sexton, Daniel Shaw, Mark Schumacher, Betty and Joel Siegel, Harvey Smith, Ken Smith, Paula Helen Stanley, David Strahan, Nancy Vacco, and Daniel Vicko.

A note of appreciation is to Dan Calabrese, John Voulgaris, and Lisa Frantzis for permission to use the "Percy the Penguin" drawing.

Corwin Press thanks the following reviewers for their contributions to this book:

Angela Becton, Teacher Instructional Support Specialist, Johnston County Schools, Smithfield, NC

Debbie Ernestberger, Library Media Specialist, East Elementary School, Murray, KY

Aaron Faletto, Music Teacher/Band Director, Bellevue School District, Bellevue, WA

Gerald A. Juhnke, Professor, University of Texas at San Antonio, San Antonio, TX

Frank Parajes, Professor, Division of Educational Studies, Emory University, Atlanta, GA

Leile Poppleton, Family and Consumer Sciences Teacher, Twin Falls High School, Twin Falls, ID

Anne Richards, Professor Emerita, University of West Georgia, Carrollton, GA

Rebecca Rupert, Teacher, Aurora Alternative High School, Bloomington, IN

Mark Sadler, Fifth-Grade Teacher, Oliver J. Kendall Elementary, Naperville, IL

John J. Schmidt, Professor of Counselor Education, East Carolina University, Greenville, NC

Ken Smith, Counseling and Educational Psychologist, Trescowthick School of Education, Australian Catholic University, Fitzroy, Victoria, Australia

Paula Helen Stanley, Professor, Counselor Education Department, Radford University, Radford, VA

About the Author

 **William Watson Purkey** is Professor Emeritus of Counselor Education at the University of North Carolina at Greensboro and cofounder of the International Alliance for Invitational Education. The alliance is a nonprofit educational group dedicated to creating and maintaining truly welcoming schools.

William was born in Shenandoah, Virginia, and went on to become a U.S. Senate page boy, soda jerk, theater usher, lifeguard, bookstore clerk, fish store manager, railroad yard clerk, gandy dancer, U.S. national park ranger, junior high school teacher, explosive ordnance disposal specialist in the U.S. Air Force, and tenured full professor at two major universities.

In addition to receiving the Board of Governors' Award for Excellence in Teaching, the highest award for teaching given by the University of North Carolina System, he also received the 2005 Excellence in Education Award presented by the Royal Conservatory of Music for his work in encouraging learning through the arts.

William's mission in life is to invite others to laugh, learn, and live fully. He now lives in Greensboro, North Carolina, with Imogene, his bride of fifty-four years.

**CORWIN
PRESS**

The Corwin Press logo—a raven striding across an open book—represents the union of courage and learning. Corwin Press is committed to improving education for all learners by publishing books and other professional development resources for those serving the field of PreK–12 education. By providing practical, hands-on materials, Corwin Press continues to carry out the promise of its motto: **"Helping Educators Do Their Work Better."**

Appreciating
Class Clowns

Why's everybody always pickin' on me?

> —"Charlie Brown" by Jerry Leiber
> and Mike Stoller, Tiger Music, Inc., 1959

INTRODUCTION

Allow me to present my credentials for writing this book about class clowns. My first qualification is that I have conducted research on class clowns and have studied the lives of professional comedians while serving as a professor of educational psychology at the University of Florida and a professor of counselor education at the University of North Carolina at Greensboro.

My second qualification is that I am a certified class clown. I can never remember a time when I was not a class clown. I have spent my life pursuing laughter. I realized I was hooked on laughter when at four years of age I found a rubber pretend knife. This great find allowed me to develop my specialty act, an "Indian dance" (with apologies to First Nations and other Native Americans). Although I had never seen an Indian dance and knew nothing about dancing, I became a local celebrity. Adults asked me to do my Indian dance. I happily obliged.

My willingness to perform was more than an attention-seeking process. I needed to share something I considered precious with others. This something was a most cordial and sincere summons to laugh and live fully, if only for a moment.

One of my earliest Indian dance solo performances was during my grandmother's Eastern Star Chapter meeting of twenty elderly ladies. My performance featured me in my underpants, dancing madly, making silly noises, showing a frightening face, and brandishing my rubber dagger. Getting attention was my life's blood. It meant attention, acceptance, and perhaps even love.

Then came school. I went first class in first grade. I learned to read by sounding out dirty words on bathroom walls. There I discovered the magic of double entendre. My word was "but," and it was as close to risqué as I could imagine. Whenever the teacher's back was turned, I scurried to the next row of desks and whispered "but" in the ear of the first-grade class beauty. This behavior brought the house down . . . with me under it. I failed first grade. The teacher said I was too immature. She was probably right.

Then, my chosen career as class clown picked up speed. I went solo theater. I did anything for laughs. Receiving attention meant everything, even at the cost of punishment. Through elementary school, I spent so much time in the principal's office that I practically became the assistant principal.

During my frequent visits to the principal's office for being "out of line," I systematically befriended the school secretary, Miss Savage. I cheerfully volunteered to sharpen pencils, collate papers, stuff envelopes, staple handbooks, dust shelves, count books, empty trashcans, track down the custodian, and do any dog work that needed to be done. These efforts paid off handsomely. I became the school secretary's pet (she could not afford a dog).

My favorite tasks were to run errands and deliver messages. These tasks required a hall permit, which was the ultimate "Get Out of Jail Free" card. Delivering a note to someone in the school provided me with endless opportunities to practice my chosen profession as class clown.

My greatest joy was to return to the classroom from which I had most recently been ejected. I would peek through the oblong window in the classroom door and wait until the teacher's back was turned. When my classmates spotted me, I would present my "Indian" face. The teacher would be completely puzzled by the outburst of student laughter. Then, she would turn quickly and catch my Indian face framed in the window. About this time, I was introduced to ISS—in-school suspension.

The ISS room was located in a converted coal bin in the school basement. It was the elementary school equivalent to a maximum-security prison. I survived quite nicely in the coal bin, plotting ways to gain future attention. I considered my time in the coal bin as "between engagements."

My role as class clown blossomed in secondary school. Jefferson Senior High was a large school that served all of the high school students in Roanoke, Virginia. There I joined the Jefferson marching band as a drummer. This offered fresh opportunities for clowning. One day during band class, the director, Mr. Jerry White, made the mistake of leaving the band room to take a phone call. After he left, I convinced the eighty band members to line up four abreast and march down the wide hallways of Jefferson Senior High (while all classes were in session), playing "Stars and Stripes Forever." I may have been one of the reasons for the principal's early retirement.

Many of my happiest moments as a class clown took place in the cavernous Jefferson Senior High auditorium. There I participated in the French Class Assembly Program. Geraldine Leftwich (fellow student and a delightful free spirit) and I shocked everyone with a risqué Apache dance that included a lit cigarette and a split skirt. We were not enrolled in the French class, and we had never seen an Apache dance. Such barriers meant little in my endless quest for laughter.

In that same cavernous auditorium, before the entire student body, I participated in the American Legion Extemporaneous Oratorical Contest. Students who entered were expected to study the United States Constitution prior to the contest. On stage, each student contestant would reach in a hat and pull out a slip of paper. Each slip contained the title of one of the articles of the Constitution. Each contestant was given seven minutes to speak about the article he or she drew.

I do not remember which article I pulled from the hat, but it made no difference. I had not read the United States Constitution. However, I had read a story about Nathan Hale, who was an early American patriot. During the Revolutionary War, he was captured by the British and hanged without trial. That information was all a true class clown, in a state of panic, needed. I began my seven-minute speech declaring my love for freedom and my appreciation of American patriots. Then, I switched my assigned U.S. Constitution article to Nathan Hale. Even here I faced a challenge. I could not remember what I had read about Nathan Hale, other than the British hanged him for spying. To fill my allotted seven minutes, I described Nathan's slow climb up the gallows steps—one (pause), two (pause), three, (long pause), four (longer pause), five (looong pause). My fellow students immediately recognized what I was up to and began to assist me with my very slow count. I reached the twelfth step of the gallows just as the required seven minutes elapsed. There are times when desperate wit is stronger than academic knowledge or platform skill. I won the contest.

My college life was more of the same. There I learned how to yawn with my mouth closed. On a bet, I wheeled the college homecoming queen around the entire campus perimeter in a wheelbarrow. With the help of a few fellow clowns, I delivered a 200-pound pig up a fire escape to the top floor of the girls' dorm. Later, I started a water fight in the dorm that resulted in considerable water damage (for which we paid dearly).

Sharing my early life as a certified class clown is not to gloat over a misspent youth. Rather, it is to establish my credentials for writing this book. I am proud to be a class clown. The greatest gift I know is to bring laughter to fellow human beings.

THE CASE FOR CLASS CLOWNS

Before making a case for class clowns, it is important to acknowledge that clowns can be a royal pain in the . . . neck. Clowns are far more likely than nonclowns to talk back, get out of line, push boundaries, and disrupt class.

As a former junior high school teacher, I have lived with the harshest of realities regarding clown misbehavior. Yet class clowns, when their energy and humor are properly channeled, can be a delightful presence in any classroom.

Here is how Tom Sexton, a veteran of almost four decades in the classroom, described his experiences with class clowns:

> I learned over the decades that if a teacher is fortunate enough to find a student with a great sense of humor, the smart thing to do is to tap into that rare gift and celebrate it. The energy that student humor brings to the class is priceless and helps to create an inviting classroom for everyone. Sometimes this humor needs to be managed by the teacher, as kids can get too caught up in it. However, it is a mistake for the teacher to squash it, as so many teachers tend to do. I have had students with this gift of humor and they have made the entire school year so much more enjoyable for the entire class.

Joel Siegel, special friend and classic class clown, provided this sample of funny business. When his third-grade teacher asked him to use the word "terrain" in a sentence, he responded, "It looks like it's going to rain." A class clown's comic attitude, when properly channeled, is truly a class treasure.

Seldom before in American history has there been a greater need for cheerfulness. Discontent, dissatisfaction, disappointment, frustration, and anger permeate our society. We are presently living through what many consider a humorless, reactionary, hate-filled moment in history.

Schools in particular seem to be locked in a mean-spirited approach to education. Zero tolerance, high-stakes testing, uniform standards, Procrustean curriculum, mandatory retention, drug-free zones, fear of violence, constant surveillance, metal detectors, shake-down searches, rigid dress codes, and ruthless competition leave little time for laughter, joy, and cheerfulness for students, educators, and support staff.

To illustrate the uptight and often illogical anxieties of public education, one school introduced two new programs during the same year. The first was a comprehensive drug-testing program. The second was a program to "just say no" to drugs. Students who "just said no" to the drug testing were promptly expelled.

Perhaps never before in North American history has there been a greater need for schools to lighten up. Perhaps never before has there been such a great need for humor, laughter, and cheerfulness in the classroom.

An unappreciated and often unrecognized source of humor, laughter, and cheerfulness is found in almost every classroom. This source is the wit and humor of class clowns. The class clowns' lighthearted and often upside down, loopy approach to life helps to banish the boredom, gloom, and monotony that can demoralize any classroom or school. Class clowns can provide sunshine for both the mind and the heart.

Here is how a second-grade class clown contributed to fun and laughter. Just before the Thanksgiving holiday recess a teacher asked her class, "What are we thankful for this Thanksgiving?" The little clown instantly replied, "I'm thankful I'm not a turkey!"

The laughter triggered by class clowns can have a significant impact on the psychological and even the physical well-being of teachers and students. Laughter allows us to accept the reality of stressful situations, while seeking ways to deal with adversity. It encourages us to make the best of embarrassing situations. Claudia Cornett, in her book *Learning Through Laughter* (2001), offers a long list of reasons for embracing humor in the educative process.

Betty Prescott, former principal of a junior high school, shared an embarrassing moment that illustrates the value of humor in schools:

> I met with all six classes of my junior high students before they left on a field trip to the Biltmore House in Asheville, North Carolina. I gave them the usual speech: "You are a representative of our school. You want to bring honor to our school, so behave like ladies and gentlemen—no foolishness." At that moment a "balloon" came floating down the aisle. I took this opportunity to say, "See, this is exactly what I'm talking about! We will not have students playing with balloons on the bus during our trip." I picked up the balloon, raised my chin and exited the room with dignity. I walked straight to my secretary's desk and asked, "This isn't a balloon, is it?" As she laughed hysterically, she confirmed my suspicion— the "balloon" was an inflated prophylactic. You have to love junior high kids to live with them!

A number of scientific studies (see Seligman, 2002) indicate that a sense of humor, measured by the Multi-dimensional Sense of Humor Scale (MSHS), relates positively to a number of factors associated with psychological health. These factors include optimism, self-esteem, and perceived physical health. Negative scores on the MSHS are associated with psychological distress and depression. Good humor and laughter seem to be intimately related to one's quality of life. This includes having fun.

HAVING FUN AS A TEACHING STRATEGY

A significant advantage of humor is that it can be a super teaching instrument. It can be used to teach concepts and stimulate intellectual development. Canada's Royal Conservatory of Music has developed an exciting, fun-filled program titled Learning Through the Arts. This program features such creative strategies as learning math through dance, science through music, language through rhythm, and social studies through visual arts. The goal is to integrate the arts into all content areas.

One high school teacher uses the television comedy show *Gilligan's Island* to teach history, government, literature, and sociology. She points out that *Gilligan's Island* was inspired by Daniel Defoe's *Robinson Crusoe*. The comic characters serve to represent a microcosm of American society. Each of the seven represents a segment of humanity. The teacher tosses out trivia questions to capture student interest: "What did Mary Ann do for a living before she was shipwrecked?" "Where did Gilligan sleep?" "What was the Skipper's pet name for Gilligan?" "Why did the seven characters pack so much luggage for a three-hour trip?" "Why, with so much talent, could they not figure a way to leave the island?" The class session ended with students singing the theme song that explains what the seven were doing on the island in the first place.

By using *Gilligan's Island* as a fun-filled stimulus, the teacher encourages communication and dialogue among her students. Education itself is a sort of dialogue. Dialogue assumes different viewpoints and opinions. Class clowns are quick to enter into dialogue with fellow students and teachers, particularly when they have the opportunity to have fun.

An illustration of how to teach math by having fun was provided by Lise Bourgeois at Fredericton's George Street Middle School. Lise instructs her eighth-grade students to construct paper airplanes for a math unit on data management. She asks her students to take five different trials of the same plane and measure the distance it flew. The students then calculate the mean, median, and mode of the average distances and plot the results on a graph. Lise explained that by having students actually see the plane in flight, they can understand why graphs look the way they do.

Over and above its value as a teaching strategy, having fun has value in its own right. It need not be justified solely on its association with school achievement. To paraphrase a hit song, "Students just want to have fun." Funny happenings reduce everyday tensions and frustrations, while making life more enjoyable. When one class clown was asked to name the longest river in South America, he replied, "It's not in South America." This particular clown delighted in loopy answers. When asked how many degrees in a circle, he asked, "How big is the circle?"

Jack Handey, a super class clown, told this tale: "I guess of all my uncles, I liked Uncle Caveman the best. We called him Uncle Caveman because he lived in a cave and because sometimes he'd eat one of us. Later on, we found out he was a bear." What teacher can resist such upside-down thinking?

Breeding Ground for Professional Comedians

There are many opportunities for class clowns to become professional comedians. The fast-paced, nutty fraternity of show business is always on the lookout for talented youngsters. This talent is evident even before the class clown becomes a teenager. Steve Allen, in his book *The Funny Men* (1968), suggested that if a child is not a class clown by the time he or she is twelve years of age, it is highly unlikely that the child will ever develop into a professional comedian.

With very few exceptions, professional comedians began their careers as class clowns. From early childhood, class clowns possess an almost indefinable and spontaneous spark that separates them from the rest of society. This spark appears very early in life. Those who possess this ability are endowed with a rare and precious gift. Joan Rivers, professional comedian, referred to this talent as a gift from the gods.

Class clowns rarely tell jokes that require a narrative setup (e.g., "Have you heard the one about . . .). For class clowns, joke telling is least important in creating laughter. Rather, most class clowns depend on observational humor and lightning-fast rejoinders and one-liners. For example, when one Virginia teacher asked her class to name Thomas Jefferson's final home, a class clown instantly answered, "I bet heaven." It would be hard to take issue with such an insightful response.

A clown's sense of humor seems spontaneous, achieved in the absence of previous conscious thought. Malcolm Gladwell, author of *Blink: The Power of Thinking Without Thinking* (2004) describes the snap, quick-as-a-wink actions made on the basis of intuition rather than information. These actions often take the form of a sudden explosion of funny comments, representing lightning calculations that put seemingly unrelated things together.

To illustrate, when one young teacher was establishing rules of behavior at the beginning of the school year, she announced to her third-grade class, "If you need to go to the bathroom, please raise your hand." The resident class clown responded, "How's that gonna help?" Clowns are quick to notice the similarity of things that differ, and the differences of things that are alike.

In the martial arts, when thought and action happen spontaneously, it is called sparking. Here is how Milton Berle (1989), a classic stand-up comedian, describes an early sparking experience:

> I was about four when I tossed off my first ad lib. My Uncle Charlie was at the dinner table with us. My Uncle Charlie had a unique way of going at chicken soup. In his hands, the soupspoon was a baton. The golden globules of fat in the steaming broth were notes to be tossed out in all directions. On this occasion, my mother cautioned Uncle Charlie to eat neatly, saying, "If you get one stain on that shirt, I'll kill you." I chimed in. I said, "Momma, you better kill Poppa. It's his shirt." My brothers laughed. Uncle Charlie laughed. My father laughed. My mother debated a comeuppance but decided what the hell, and she laughed too. (p. xxii)

A class clown's humorous talent exhibits itself early, even before the first days in school. Evidence of a class clown's intangible and almost ephemeral spark is found in the early lives of famous comedians. By the time he was three years old, Jack Benny was collecting all of the chairs in his home and placing them in rows. Then, he would put on his show, reciting poems, telling stories, and singing nursery rhymes. Milton Berle was tossing out one-liners before he was sixty months old. Bob Hope demonstrated his remarkable ability to make people laugh by the time he was four years of age. Andy Kaufman and Steve Martin began performing for fun by the time they were five years of age. Bernie Mac learned how to make his mother laugh through her tears when he was only five.

When clowns enter school, they are already in love with laughter. Tim Conway was breaking classmates up in kindergarten. Nine-year-old Jerry Lewis was getting laughs in his elementary school. Jerry Seinfeld was writing a book about humor while still a young boy. Bill Maher knew he wanted to be a professional comedian by the age of ten. George Carlin wrote in his fifth-grade yearbook that he wanted to be a professional comedian when he grew up. Before he dropped out, Chris Rock kept everyone in his school laughing.

An example of a class clown starting young is Jay Leno, stand-up comic and television show host. In his book *Leading with My Chin* (1996), he describes what a teacher wrote on his fifth-grade report card: "Jay has the ability, but does not apply himself." Jay explained that the only time his mind was totally focused and not spinning all over the map looking for distraction was when he was being funny. From early on, Jay's greatest goal in life was to make people laugh.

Many class clowns go on to become internationally famous comedians and comedy writers. This was especially true during the late twentieth century "Golden Age" of comedy, when many class clowns became professional comedians. These include Steve Allen, Lucille Ball, Jack Benny, Milton Berle, Lenny Bruce, George Burns, Sid Caesar, Johnny Carson, Imogene Coco, Phyllis Diller, Dick Gregory, Bob Hope, Jerry Lewis, Richard Pryor, Joan Rivers, Red Skelton, and Jonathan Winters, among others. Many of these classic comedians are still with us and continue to be highly popular.

We now have a new generation of gifted comedians to make us laugh. This group includes David Chappelle, Margaret Cho, Billy Crystal, Ellen DeGeneres, Whoopi Goldberg, Kathy Griffin, Darrell Hammond, Steve Harvey, Jay Leno, George Lopez, Bernie Mac, Eddie Murphy, Conan O'Brien, Rita Rudner, Jerry Seinfeld, Jon Stewart, Chris Rock, Wanda Sykes, Robin Williams, and many others too numerous to mention. But whether classic or contemporary, professional comedians report an early background of having been class clowns. They sensed at an early age that clowning was what they were uniquely suited for and what they were put on this earth to do.

Jerry Lewis, world famous comedian, wrote that everyone who walks out on a stage is a child. He explained that they're out there for one reason—to gain affection and understanding. For Jerry Lewis, applause means "I love you, baby," "Good job, sweetheart."

Here is a story told by Tim Conway to describe his early life as a class clown:

In kindergarten class, PS 149, Miss Delaney tells us we've got to act out the story of Thanksgiving. It's all about John Alden and Miles Standish and eating turkeys and sweet potatoes. I've never eaten this stuff, and I don't know who these guys are, but I figure if she says John Alden first, he must be the big shot.

"I wanna be John Alden!" I yell. I am put in the pilgrim chorus. All we have to do is walk across the stage, carrying a cardboard musket. And Miss Delaney warns us, "If you don't bring your own costume, you're not in the play."

Okay. Pop is a skilled tinsmith. Working from a picture in the *Jewish Daily Forward*, he wraps some five-and-dime-store black oilcloth around an old derby to look like a stovepipe and attaches a belt buckle to the front of the hat with thin iron wire.

Two days later: As I walk across the stage with the motley pilgrims, I stop and scream, "Oh! The Indians!" I grab my heart, as if hit by an arrow, and fall down. Gasps in the auditorium.

Then I jump up, smile at the people so they'll know I'm not hurt. And I amble off. In the hall, Miss Delaney grabs my ear, and her huge bosom trembles menacingly over my eyes: "You bad boy! Why couldn't you just walk across like I told you?"

I don't know why. I had to make a production out of it. I had to be "on."

Few class clowns go on to become professional comedians, but all clowns contribute to a more cheerful world. Regardless of what adult occupations or professions class clowns find themselves in, they are usually successful. Alleen and Don Nilsen, in their book *Encyclopedia of 20th-Century American Humor* (2000), state that there are few if any careers where having a sense of humor would not contribute to personal and professional success.

Who Is a Class Clown?

A class clown is a student who consistently and successfully invites laughter. Class clowns' humor is an affirmation of cheerfulness and a declaration of the human spirit. Class clowns are able to express with humor what often is implied or unsaid. They are usually the ones who take the first step and utter a new word. They inspirit and inspire us with their cheerfulness and love of life.

A special quality of class clowns is to combine humor with metaphors. Class clowns have the capacity to paint new realities using funny and often mixed metaphors and similes. Willie Cosh, a Scottish friend and very funny guy, provided an example: "The world is your lobster." Another fun-filled example is the comment of a class clown who responded to an insult: "I may be an idiot, but at least I'm not smart."

People think in pictures. Class clowns sense this and exploit it by drawing funny cartoon worlds with words. Ann Nivens, an elementary school administrator, provided an example of a clown's tendency to think in terms of pictures. Ann said that when she was in the sixth grade her class moved from room to room for math, English, social studies, and science. Ann's classmate was Bucky, an unflappable class clown. The sixth-grade

English teacher was extremely demanding. She had the reputation of being the meanest teacher in the whole school. Students were afraid to even whisper in her classroom. Bucky, on the other hand, took life in stride. To him, everything was a joke. He was full of fun and laughter. The English teacher assigned the class to write a thousand-word essay. Bucky turned in his paper, which contained a single drawing. Under the drawing Bucky wrote that his social studies teacher said that a picture was worth a thousand words.

Class clowns differ from circus clowns, who rely on outlandish costumes, grotesque makeup, and physical abnormalities. Class clowns, on the other hand, generally rely on their wit, humor, and zany personalities. In school, Jerry Lewis was constantly doing off-the-wall things. His classmates called him "Id" for idiot.

In writing about circus clowns, Jack Handey (1992), a professional comedian and former class clown, explained that for him circus clowns aren't funny. He wondered where his fear of clowns started, and he concluded that his fear goes back to the time he went to a circus and a clown killed his dad. There is a fine madness in the zany statements of many class clowns that is hard to resist.

Both class clowns and circus clowns delight in working with a partner, often covering each other with meringue pies, real or imagined. This dialogue was heard between two high school class clowns. The first said to his partner, "That guy looks like our principal." The second clown responded, "That is the principal." The first clown commented, "Well, they certainly resemble each other."

As every teacher knows, the natural habitat of class clowns is schools. Schools have always provided a rich environment where class clowns can sharpen their skills at making people laugh. Classrooms, cafeterias, playgrounds, athletic fields, bathrooms, hallways, and auditoriums all provide a performance stage and a captive audience. When a middle school teacher admonished her class, "When I was your age, I could name all of the presidents in order," a quick-witted clown responded, "That's not fair. There were only four when you were our age." Class clowns have a constant supply of funny material and an appreciative audience of fellow students.

The ability to make others laugh seems to be instinctive. Viewing class clown behavior as instinctive is not meant to open the age-old debates between nature and nurture, heredity and environment. ("If a child looks like his dad, that's heredity. If he looks like a neighbor, that's environment.") Rather, instinctive is meant to suggest a predisposing talent for making people laugh. Martin Seligman (2002) uses the term "signature strengths" to describe strengths of character. A signature strength of class clowns is a comic attitude toward life. Who could ever forget Jon Stewart's bemused look or Oliver Hardy's slow burn? This gift for laughter is triggered and maintained by early life experiences.

Often the trigger is an older relative who serves as a role model. The model is usually a funny adult who is greatly admired by the emerging class clown. Jay Leno reported that his father had a profound impact on him because of his dad's zany attitude toward life.

In my own role as class clown, my role model was my mother. She had a wonderful *Auntie Mame* approach to life that filled the world with laughter. In her last days on earth, she prepared a sign for her hospice room door: "I may be depleted, but I'm not defeated."

We all can be witty on occasion, but we cannot match class clowns whose wit comes from some hidden power. Class clowns have an unmistakably funny personality, coupled with a humorous outlook on life. Sheldon

Patinkin (2000), author of *The Second City: Backstage at the World's Greatest Comedy Theater,* described clowns this way: "What may define Second City clowns most clearly is that they're the ones audiences start laughing at by the second time they see them on the show, regardless of what's happening in the scene." As Patinkin explained, being a class clown isn't anything that can be taught. Trying to be funny is like trying to be a giant. You can pretend to be serious, but it is very difficult to pretend to be a class clown. It's part of your personality, your charisma, your sense of yourself, and you carry it with you where ever you go. No matter what a class clown says or does, it tends to be funny. While the currency of clowns is laughter, cheerfulness is their commodity.

THE VALUE OF CHEERFULNESS

Cheerfulness is a quality of good spirit, joy, optimism, and gladness that warms the hearts of most people. According to the Renaissance scholar Michel de Montaigne, "The highest wisdom is continual cheerfulness; such a state, like the region above the moon, is always clear and serene." Cheerfulness differs from happiness, which is a consistent feeling of well-being and contentment. Class clowns may not be happy, but they are of good spirit, the life of the party. There is life to be enjoyed, and they want to be a part of it. Their cheerfulness seems to brighten a room when they enter and darken it when they leave. They follow Shakespeare's advice in *Richard II*, "Lay aside life-harming heaviness and entertain a cheerful disposition." For class clowns, being serious is equivalent to being dull. Perhaps the most serious conviction a class clown holds is that nothing is to be taken too seriously.

The words "cheer" and "cheerful" have a rich history. In the *King James Bible* the terms appear often. However, in later translations (*The Complete Bible: An American Translation*, 2001) "cheer" and "cheerful" were changed to "courage" and "courageous." It is interesting to note that *cor*, the Latin word for "heart," is the basis for the word "courage." Both cheer and courage are invitations to take heart and be of good spirit. Both terms describe the upbeat approach to life exhibited by most class clowns.

To conclude this introduction to class clowns, clowns are sometimes referred to as "devilish." This term is usually used in a generally affectionate way. Devilishness is typically exhibited in the form of practical jokes, mischievous pranks, satirical comments, and harmless tricks. However, there is always the danger that if devilishness goes too far it can result in the clown's humor becoming hostile.

Claudia Cornett (2001), a noted authority on learning through laughter, offers this caution:

> Humor does have its dangers, and it is the wise teacher who knows its force. If it occurs at the wrong moment or is inappropriate, it can destroy a mood or distract attention. If it gets out of hand, it can turn a classroom into a circus. And if it ridicules (like sarcasm), feelings can be hurt. Humor can belittle and denigrate, leaving the recipient feeling powerless. (p. 46)

The ability to monitor and control the social environment is a hallmark of good teaching.

Class clowns teach us to laugh at ourselves. Laughter is a wonderful safety valve. It is the ability to laugh at the mistakes we make. Teachers who cannot see the humor in much of what happens in school are in danger of what educators call burnout. Teachers who cannot laugh are dangerous to themselves and dangerous to their students. Chapter 2 explains the two basic types of class clowns and shows how these types influence life in classrooms.

ENCORE

(A REAPPEARANCE AND ADDITIONAL PERFORMANCE)

1. Have Fun. Humor is a wonderful teaching strategy. It can teach concepts and stimulate intellectual development. Moreover, humor has value in its own right. It need not be justified solely on its positive connections with academic achievement.

Suggestion: Make a list of ways that you have fun and check the list regularly. Enjoying physical activities, reading books, meeting with friends, spending time with loved ones, and traveling to exciting places are just the tip of the iceberg on ways to invite fun and laughter into your life. Make sure you're not shortchanging yourself.

2. Channel Humor. When classroom fun is not properly channeled, it becomes a disruptive force. The teacher's ability to monitor and control the classroom social environment is a hallmark of good teaching.

Suggestion: Most books on classroom management stress six important teacher practices: dress better than your students, provide successful experiences for everyone, plan lessons ahead, keep your cool, be consistent, and be professional.

3. Inspirit Your School. School can become more welcoming, lighthearted, and enjoyable for everyone who enters the building. Class clowns help banish boredom, fight monotony, and spread sunshine.

Suggestion: Talk to colleagues about having the first five minutes of every school meeting devoted to "happy talk." Share successes, tell funny stories, sing a humorous school song, do a skit. Do what it takes to invite everyone to lighten up.

Understanding
Class Clowns

Look, he's winding up the watch of his wit,
By and by it will strike.

> —William Shakespeare, *The Tempest*

*O*n average, there is likely to be one class clown in each group of thirty-five students. (In class clown research I conducted with Sandra Damico, we identified 96 class clowns among 3,500 eighth-grade students; Damico & Purkey, 1979). For teachers, these clowns can be an invitation to heaven or to hell.

There is no question that class clowns can have a powerful negative influence in any classroom. They have probably been the bane of teachers since the beginning of civilization. Countless teachers have probably abandoned teaching because of the behavior of class clowns. Actions that seem funny to class clowns can be hurtful, disrespectful, disruptive, and insulting. There are times when clowning can get out of hand and need not be tolerated.

Being a successful teacher of class clowns does not require martyrdom. Class clowns will sometimes violate the most reasonable and appropriate rules. When such disruptions occur, appropriate penalties are necessary. Penalties, such as denial of privileges, should be used sparingly. They should be applied with an attitude of respect for the clown and sadness at the offense. Penalties should not give the clown the resentful feeling of being wronged.

Clowns can also have a wonderfully positive influence, as indicated in Chapter 1. But whether positive or negative, class clowns are here and are likely to stay. This book helps teachers make the best of it by transforming and steering clown energy into a classroom asset.

HUMOR BRAIN DRAIN

In the past, schools suffered a tremendous loss of class clown talent. This loss continues to occur, as evidenced by the dropout rate of many young comics. The tension between educators and class clowns may explain why many class clowns who go on to become professional comedians are largely self-educated. As Mark Twain commented, "I have never let my schooling interfere with my education."

Consider this array of class clowns who dropped out of school and later became famous comedians. George Burns quit school when he was thirteen years old. Lenny Bruce ran away from home and school when barely a teenager. Jack Benny dropped out of school in the ninth grade. So did George Carlin. Chris Rock dropped out a little later. Red Skelton received little formal schooling and could hardly read. Rosie O'Donnell flunked out of college her first year. Stan Laurel ran away from home to avoid school. David Letterman's public school academic record was less than mediocre. Jay Leno described himself as "the worst student in the history of academia" (Leno, 1996). Woody Allen was expelled from New York University, Dan Aykroyd dropped out of school at age seventeen, and Henry "The Fonz" Winkler was a terrible student. In a radio interview, Winkler said that his grades were so bad that he threw himself a party when he received a C minus. The dropout rate of class clowns is disturbing. It represents a sort of comic brain drain in schools.

A major cause of schools' comic brain drain is the friction between teachers and class clowns. One reason for this friction is that many educators do not recognize that there are two types of class clowns: friendly clowns and hostile clowns. Educators can take advantage of the positive qualities of friendly clowns. They can also seek and find ways to ameliorate or redirect the negative qualities of hostile clowns.

FRIENDLY CLOWNS AND HOSTILE CLOWNS

When Sandra Damico and I (1979) conducted our class clown research at the University of Florida, we looked at student and teacher perceptions of clowns and nonclowns. We identified almost one hundred class clowns within a large population of eighth-grade students. We selected our class clowns by asking students to name a classmate who makes them laugh a lot—the class clown. Students who received more than ten peer nominations were identified as clowns. Some students received twenty or more nominations. Comparisons between clowns and nonclowns (those not receiving nominations) were made on the basis of self-reports, teacher surveys, interviews, and questionnaires.

We found that there tends to be two types of class clowns. We named them "friendly clowns" and "hostile clowns." The two types overlap so much that it is difficult to tell where one ends and the other begins. The difference is more of degree than of kind. For example, the classic Three Stooges comedy team was both friendly and hostile. However, there does seem to be a divergence of clowning behavior into those two camps.

An interesting sidelight to our findings was that many teachers fail to recognize the contributions of humor made by friendly clowns. Some teachers tend to classify humor as disruptive, without recognizing the many positive ways clowning behavior can be used to accomplish learning goals. To illustrate, when one middle school teacher asked the resident class clown to name two pronouns, the clown responded, "Who, me?" Fortunately, many of the best teachers understand and appreciate that a class clown's humor can be a significant factor in making classrooms and schools more enjoyable and inviting places for everyone.

A critical ingredient in working successfully with class clowns is to get to know them. This requires personalized attention and long-term relationships. Clowns are far more likely to be a beneficial presence in the classroom when they believe they are understood and appreciated. The bottom line is that successful teachers of class clowns get results through relationships.

Friendly Clowns

Friendly clowns are well liked by classmates because they tend to make fun of themselves. Their jokes are on them, and funny things happen to them. Friendly clowns run into imaginary doors, take pratfalls, roll their eyes, make funny faces, create faux pas, make witty comments, generally act goofy, and laugh at themselves. They tend to be playful in facing difficult challenges. Their sharp intellect is often hidden behind goofy behavior. Classmates describe friendly class clowns in positive terms.

The friendly class clown's sharp intellect is often accompanied by an almost childlike innocence. When one clown decided to play hooky, he called the school secretary and explained, "Johnny can't come to school today because he's not feeling well." When the secretary asked who was calling, the clown replied, "This is my brother."

Friendly clowns demonstrate a pattern of rebellion and nonconformity, including skipping school and breaking school rules. However, their tendency to be different from "normal" students is modified by their respect for feelings. Unlike hostile clowns, making fun of physical impairments and being cruel are not part of their repertoire.

A good example of a friendly clown who became a lovable professional comedian is Red Skelton. From his "Guzzler's Gin" routine to his "Mean Little Kid" act, Red was always gentle, kind, and sensitive to feelings. He closed each one of his dozens of television programs with a simple message of friendship: "God Bless." Today, Bill Cosby, Bob Newhart, and Ellen DeGeneres demonstrate the qualities of a friendly class clown. Their delightful humor is directed toward their own tribulations and the human condition. They carefully avoid being offensive.

Hostile Clowns

Hostile class clowns have a blend of personality characteristics. They can be threatening, even frightening, and at the same time impishly funny. You never know what you're going to get. While often endearing, hostile class clowns tend to get their laughs from ridiculing and making fun of fellow students and teachers.

A colleague of mine, Bob Chappell, superintendent of Rappahannock County Schools in Virginia, offered a good example of the hostile clown. Bob said that as a young teacher he coached ninth grade basketball. During a faculty-versus-student basketball game, one of his players dropped Bob's gym shorts. Everyone thought it was funny, except Bob. Few things are as painful as being ridiculed. Bob thought it was immaturity on the part of the player, but I think it represented the player's hostile intent.

In the case of having one's gym shorts pulled down by someone who is trying to be funny, the victim is being doubly punished. First, the victim feels the pressure to laugh at the insulting behavior to demonstrate that he or she has a sense of humor. (Defenders of the student's behavior would proclaim, "It was only a joke!") The second punishment is that the victim is often denied the chance to respond directly to the highly embarrassing action (e.g., knocking the student's head off).

There is a sadistic undercurrent in hostile clowns. They flip books being carried under the arms of fellow students, yank chairs from under people, and mimic and ridicule physical characteristics. They often use their gift of humor as a weapon to bully people and embarrass individuals. Their ability to make people laugh is often based on ridicule, sarcasm, and hostility.

Hostile clowns have a built-in audience of many children, teenagers, and young adults who view boorishness and outrageous social behavior as hilarious. The audience enables the hostile clown to act with impunity. The hostile clown's humor is an act of slash-and-burn defiance to responsible social behavior.

Some hostile clowns, such as Andrew Dice Clay and Sam Kinison, develop into wildly successful professional comedians. Don Rickles is a good example. He has been referred to as the father of insult comedy. His razor-sharp witticisms, combined with a lovable personality, provide cover for a rather brutal attack on personal dignity. Rickles often receives laughs because his humor defies politeness and courtesy. Rickles can be impish and endearing, yet his humor can be about as compassionate as a bayonet.

An even more striking example of a hostile clown is John Belushi of *Animal House* fame. According to a colleague, Belushi is remembered for his total defiance of social responsibility. His defiance was evidenced by his overt aggression on a nationally televised talk show. Without cause or warning, Belushi threw a glass of water on another guest and kicked a coffee table over, destroying the host's favorite potted plant. John Belushi was a mixture of childlike sweetness and unbridled hostility.

As noted earlier, some people prefer hostile humor, but it can get old in a hurry. Anarchy may be temporarily hilarious (as evidenced by the early comedy films of the Marx Brothers), but it is incompatible with a democratic, decent, and caring society. Hostile class clowns who employ aggressive humor may get laughs, but over time their hostile fun wears thin.

The same is true for hostile humor itself. Sometimes, attempts at humor can be unintentionally disinviting: What is meant to be funny can come across as mocking and even cruel. Consider these comments, posted to office doors and placed on desks:

You have obviously mistaken me for someone who cares.

Have a nice day, somewhere else.

If there's a price on your head, take it.

What part of NO don't you understand?

Stupidity is not a handicap; park somewhere else.

The next time you're passing by, keep going.

Come on in, everything else has gone wrong today.

What were you when you were alive?

My cow died, so I don't need your bull.

I'd like to help you out. Which way did you come in?

If I said something to insult you, please believe me.

I got out of bed for *this?*

Please leave and let live.

The hostile class clown mentality may inadvertently appear in this book from time to time. If so, I apologize in advance. (Friendly clowns are quick to apologize for hurting someone's feelings. Hostile clowns seldom apologize.) This book is written from the perspective of a friendly class clown.

CLASS CLOWN RELATIONSHIPS

An interesting finding from our research (Damico & Purkey, 1979) was that class clowns in general maintained more negative attitudes toward teachers and principals than did nonclowns. One reason for the negative attitudes is that students value humor more highly than do teachers (Willis, 1997). "School is a rat race," commented one class clown. "Even when you win, you're still a rat."

For the most part, class clowns tend to be very bright. Abigail Sullivan Moore (2005) described how to identify gifted children. She reported that a significant characteristic of gifted children is a remarkable sense of humor. The reverse is also true. Class clowns tend to be above average in intelligence, although this intelligence shows itself in funny ways,

Clowns see themselves as willing to challenge the teacher's authority by voicing their opinions in front of classmates. As a schoolboy, Jackie Gleason ("Ralph Cramden" in *The Honeymooners*) was a constant irritant to teachers. In school, he would wait until teachers made a point, then he would stand up and challenge their facts. When the teachers became angry over Jackie's arguments, he would tell them that they were angry because they were wrong.

Craig Ferguson, professional comedian and host of CBS's *The Late, Late Show,* dropped out of high school when he was sixteen years old. This was immediately after he had a tremendous argument with his English teacher over the meaning of "existentialism." As noted earlier, the class clown's sharp intellect is often hidden beneath clever wit.

Class clowns are not timid. They do not believe everything they are told, and they don't do everything they are told to do. They see themselves as vocal leaders in expressing ideas and opinions. They are quick to assert themselves. When directly challenged, clowns can be disruptive in the most creative and ingenious ways.

My Scottish colleague, Willie Cosh, shared a story that captures the unpredictable spirit found in most clowns. A class clown, I'll call him Charlie, was offered the part of Joseph in the school nativity play but couldn't remember his lines. His teachers gave him every chance to practice and succeed, but he kept fluffing his lines. Charlie was great with spontaneous, ad-lib remarks, but he couldn't handle a script. After some diplomacy and recasting, he was given the part of the innkeeper—a non-speaking part. Charlie had only to shake his head to indicate there was no room in the inn. Charlie agreed with the change, but he was not happy about his demotion to a nonspeaking part. During the nativity scene, he couldn't help himself. When Joseph and Mary knocked on the inn door and asked, "Have you any rooms for the night?" Charlie replied, "Yes, come on in. We'll fit you in somewhere." Very few things can deter class clowns because they have a magnificent obsession to create laughter. Somber boundaries are their natural enemies.

It is not surprising that many teachers involved in our class clown research had negative views of class clowns. They described class clowns as attention seekers who are unruly, disruptive, immature, and self-centered. Here is how one educator described class clowns:

> A class clown continually disrupts the class with wisecracks, will do or say anything to be in the spotlight, doesn't know when to stop, has a response for everything that happens, and may even enjoy the attention of being corrected. The class clown constantly diverts attention, does not function on worthwhile activities, often bothers others students, and is too busy clowning to get work done in class.

The only kind comment made by the educator is that the clown may be "actually quite funny at times." The teacher concludes by suggesting that the best way to "help" the class clown is to identify the causes of his or her behavior.

Salene Cowher, a colleague and a dear friend, wrote a poem describing how a hostile school environment wore down a class clown. Here are the last two stanzas:

That One

He never fades from memory,

But you hear rumors

That he stopped trying

To be funny

Because nobody laughed.

But that one—

He did make you laugh

When you needed to laugh;

And you never did mind:

You're just so sorry

That he stopped trying.

Perhaps the negative view of class clowns held by many teachers is due to the class clown's failure to conform to contemporary ideas about behavior. Class clowns live by the rules of cheerfulness and expression, rather than the rules of somberness and conformity. The failure to conform was dramatized in Ken Kesey's novel *One Flew Over the Cuckoo's Nest* (1962). Nurse Ratched kept reminding the other hospital personnel that the asylum was for the insane, maintaining that it's important to get patients adjusted to their surroundings.

Class clowns do not adjust readily to their surroundings. For them, conformity is a procrustean nightmare. They have little patience with oppression and react quickly when they think authorities are trying to control their lives. They are also quick to spot sugar-coated demands. Doing silly things, interrupting class, and hacking around are extensions of a rebellious personality. Their behavior allows them to maintain sanity in a sometimes insane world. Mel Brooks wrote that humor is just another defense against the universe. When an elementary school teacher asked, "What is the shape of the earth?" The class clown instantly responded, "Terrible!"

Relating with others comes easy for class clowns, but their close friends are relatively few. In some odd way, class clowns are often outsiders. Class clowns take a natural, breezy, spontaneous approach to life that separates them from more "normal" students. Fellow students like class clowns. However, the clown's unpredictable role of jester prevents others from getting too close to them.

Ann Nivens provided an illustration of a class clown's quirky unpredictability. Ann is an assistant principal in Mooresville, North Carolina. She said that when she was in the fifth grade, she tossed a pencil across the room to a friend. The pencil hit the far wall with a bang just as the teacher entered the room. The teacher was furious at such misbehavior. She began to go down each row of students, asking each fifth grader, "Did you throw that pencil?" Each student declared his or her innocence.

Ann sat on the last seat in the last row. Bucky, the fifth grade class clown, sat in the seat just in front of her. (Ann knew that Bucky had a big-time crush on her.) As the teacher worked her way down the rows, asking her question to each student, Ann was in a state of panic. Just as the teacher began questioning the last row, Ann whispered in Bucky's ear, "Bucky, please tell the teacher that you threw the pencil." When the teacher finally reached Bucky (her prize suspect), she asked sternly, "Bucky, did you throw the pencil?" Bucky responded, "Nope, not me." Class clowns are unpredictable, even when they're in love.

Beyond the humor and laughter, there is a certain melancholy feeling in clowns, mixed with continuous insecurity. They may not be happy, but they manage to be cheerful. Fortunately, friendly class clowns find ways to express feelings of frustration, anger, and impatience without exploding at the slightest problem.

A good example of continuous insecurity, wrapped in false bravado, is the behavior of John Candy, a wonderfully funny comedian who is no longer with us. He was the kind of class clown who tried to hide his vulnerability. According to Sheldon Patinkin (2000), John Candy hid behind a mask of clearly fake bravery. This fake bravado may be seen in the personas of many famous comedians. Andy Kaufman, W. C. Fields, Bert Lahr, Oliver Hardy, and Bob Hope are good examples of this pretense. Who could ever forget Don Knotts, "Barney" on the *Andy Griffith Show*, warning, "My body is a weapon"? Barney was full of bluster to hide his anxiety.

Fortunately for class clowns, there are teachers, principals, and other school personnel who were class clowns themselves. These teachers relate well with their class clown students. Gorham and Christophel (1990) conducted a study of the relationship between teachers' sense of humor and student achievement. They concluded that the use of humor by teachers, including a willingness to use funny, personal examples about their lives outside the classroom, was significantly associated with student learning.

A Scottish colleague shared a description of a class clown teacher, Bob Buchanan. Bob taught interior decorating at Kibble, a large residential school for troubled youth in Glasgow, Scotland. He always signed his name "Bob Buchanan, PhD (Printer and Home Decorator)." Willie observed Bob as he handled a difficult classroom challenge. A student became frustrated with his artwork and began swearing. Bob quietly said to the student,

"Tommy, please don't swear like that. My father is up there and never liked that sort of language," while pointing to the ceiling. There was dead silence in the classroom. Finally, Tommy asked, "Is your dad in heaven?" Bob replied, "Not at all. He's on the roof stealing the lead flashings." The class rocked with laughter, including Tommy. A friend commented that watching Bob use humor and laughter to teach important subject matter was like being in the presence of a genius at work.

Another illustration of how a former class clown used his comic talents in the classroom was provided by a middle school teacher. He recalled a time when he entered his classroom to find bedlam. It was just before the Christmas holidays, and the children were wild. The teacher grabbed a ruler, slapped his desk, and shouted, "I demand chaos!" The students quickly settled down.

THE ART OF CLOWNING

According to Billy Crystal, professional comedian, "There is an art in what we do." He continued, "That's like saying Michelangelo and Jackie Mason in the same sentence. I think it's an ancient art that goes back to the first cave drawings."

Although not academic stars at school, class clowns possess a curious mind, quick intelligence, dexterity of thought, and a huge funny bone. Woody Allen sold jokes to professional comedians while he was still a schoolboy. Larry Gelbart, a prolific writer of comedy and the creator of such great stories as *A Funny Thing Happened on the Way to the Forum*; *M*A*S*H*; *Oh, God!*; and *Tootsie* was only sixteen years old when he was hired to write jokes for professional comedians.

Former class clowns, such as Carol Griffin, Chris Rock, and Eddie Murphy, have the ability to "think funny" and exhibit off beat humor. For them, studying people is more important than studying books. As one class clown commented, "I own one book in case the television breaks down."

Class clowns know that the tiniest thing can be made funny. In fact, the art of clowning, like that of a magician, remains largely invisible to the untrained eye. It does not reveal its secrets. If it is discovered that the class clown is trying to be funny, it is the kiss of death. As Larry Wilde reminds us in *How the Great Comedy Writers Create Laughter* (1976), if what you're doing is funny, you don't have to be funny doing it.

The Chinese have four tests to distinguish the greatness of art. The first is *chiao* (clever); the second, *miao* (wonderful); the third, *shen* (divine); the fourth and highest, *icho* (effortless). A good example of apparently effortless and almost invisible humor is the role of the "straight man." John Novak, a friend and very funny guy, described the comic straight man as a clown with class.

Throughout comic history, the straight man in a comedy team was always listed first in recognition of his or her importance to the act (e.g., Abbott and Costello, Burns and Allen, Martin and Lewis). Concealing one's comic ability is itself a great cleverness. As George Burns (1976), the straight man for the funny comments of Gracie Allen, explained, he became so good that nobody knew he was there. At a young age, the class clown learns to observe carefully, exaggerate slightly, and create comedy. As careful observers, class clowns often see certain realities that are hidden from nonclowns.

TRIBULATIONS OF CLASS CLOWNS

Class clowns who go on to become professional comedians often report a difficult early life, even apart from

life in classrooms. This echoes the dictum of Karl
Menninger: "Anything which can be made funny must
have at its heart some tragic implications." The comedian Lenny Bruce declared that his humor was based on
destruction and despair. Oliver Hardy, of the unforgettable comedy team Laurel and Hardy, was deeply
ashamed of his weight and cringed when he was identified as the "fat one" on the team. W. C. Fields drove himself savagely. He was never able to free himself of the
terrible poverty he experienced as a child. Mort Sahl coupled his tremendous comic talent with terrible insecuri-
ties. Fortunately, class clowns have the knack to turn
painful experiences into comedy.

The reverse is also true. Clowns excel in moving from
comedy to tragedy. There are many great dramatic performances by comedians. Jack Lemmon gave a magnificent performance in the film *Days of Wine and Roses*.
Jackie Gleason, Whoopi Goldberg, Lily Tomlin, and
Robin Williams all received international acclaim for dramatic performances. More recently, Bill Murray received
an Academy Award nomination for his remarkable performance in the film *Lost in Translation*. As the ancient
Greeks recognized, comedy and tragedy are two sides of
the same coin.

Tragedy is the raw material for comedy. Dick Gregory
(1964) was born and raised in poverty and with social
services relief. This is how he described his early life:

> The teacher thought I was a troublemaker. All she
> saw from the front of the room was a little black boy
> who squirmed in his idiot's seat and made noises
> and poked the kids around him. I guess she couldn't
> see a kid who made noises because he wanted some-
> one to know he was there. (p. 30)

Jackie Gleason's childhood was extremely painful
and poverty stricken. This poverty is a kind of privation

that is much more than economic. It is a chronic perceived deprivation of affection, accompanied by low self-esteem. This sense of inferiority may be physical, emotional, or both. Joan Rivers wrote that there is not one female comic who was beautiful as a child. In fact, with some exceptions, most comedians are not attractive in a classical sense. This perceived lack of attractiveness probably adds fuel to their humor.

Ellen DeGeneres said that she never exhibited her comic talents in school, due to shyness and chronic stage fright. However, as a child, she discovered the power of laughter in creating good energy. DeGeneres described that when her parents divorced, her mother went through a very difficult period. When Ellen saw her mother crying, she did everything she could to make her mother laugh. When her mother laughed, Ellen would imitate her mother's laughter, causing her mother to laugh even harder.

Rodney Dangerfield disclosed that his mother was thoughtless and often cruel. As a child, he rode a bus for one hour each way to see his divorced father. He made this trip two times a year. Bill Murray, master of deadpan humor, grew up in a blue-collar neighborhood, the fifth of nine children. According to one of his sisters, Bill had to learn how to get attention just to survive. Many class clowns experience continuous insecurity. They adjust to this insecurity by constantly trying to call attention to themselves.

Being a successful clown does not necessarily require unhappiness. Not all comedians are unhappy or had a painful childhood. Jerry Seinfeld considered the "sad clown" concept simply a cliché. He rejected the stereotype of Pagliacci, who makes others laugh while his heart is breaking. Yet early difficulties do seem to be a significant predisposing factor for becoming a class clown. In my own life, my father was killed when I was a young child. My stern grandmother, who raised me, disliked my father and may have transferred this dislike to me. Charles Chaplin put it this way: "Good humor is only a hairline from good tragedy." This may be why clowns have developed the ability to laugh at adversity. Again, if they can't be happy, they can at least be cheerful. This spirit of resilient cheerfulness in the face of adversity is exhibited beautifully by an unknown poet:

> Some may play the martyr
>
> While I the jester's role.
>
> But the subtle smile I wear
>
> Hides scars upon my soul.

Class clowns have a philosophy of life that may be described as pragmatic fatalism. On the one hand, class clowns believe that they are free to make a difference in their own lives. On the other hand, they resign themselves to destiny. Jean-Paul Sartre wrote that freedom is what we do with what's been done to us. The freedom of class clowns is to play the cards dealt to them by fate, particularly the joker. When one elementary school class clown was asked if she liked going to school, she responded, "Oh, yes, I like going to school, and I like coming from school. It's school I don't like."

Regardless of fortunate or unfortunate childhood experiences, clowns have a fierce desire to be the center of attention. They love to be "on." This need for attention is a powerful incentive for class clowns. Jack Benny provided a good illustration of this need. When asked why he was going to London, England, to do a one-man show, he replied, "Well, I just want to show off."

A producer who worked with Bob Hope for years stated in an interview that Bob Hope "has to get out on stage. He has to hear the applause. He has to hear the laughter. He thoroughly enjoys it. . . . For Bob, if there is no laughter, there is no life." Ellen DeGeneres described a similar approach to life. As a child growing up in New Orleans, she wanted to be famous. She felt that fame would bring attention and make her feel special.

Anyone who is a true class clown has no choice but to be funny. Class clowns are more constructive and destructive, more sane and more insane, more civilized and more primitive, more insightful and more oblivious, more endearing and more obnoxious than other human beings. Charles Chaplin, arguably the greatest comedian who ever stepped on a stage, maintained that humor allows us to see what seems important as unimportant, what seems rational as irrational. He maintained that humor was a way to maintain sanity in a sometimes insane world. The same sentiment was expressed by Mel Brooks, the comic genius of the smash Broadway hit *The Producers.*

For a clown, no more fiendish punishment could be imagined than to remain absolutely unnoticed. They hope that this notice will be in the form of approval. George Carlin described the need for attention and approval this way: "You're looking for approval every five, ten, fifteen seconds, and you're trying to sustain this approval from moment to moment to moment" (Grace, 1991, p. 21). Jay Leno (1996) said that, as a kid, he never did anything unless somebody was watching. Being in the spotlight, no matter how positive or negative, provides the clown with the feeling that he or she is worthy of attention.

The drive for attention is true of both friendly and hostile class clowns. However, the direction this drive takes them is influenced by significant others. In some cases, a class clown's early tendency toward hostility can be neutralized and counteracted by an "antitoxin" adult who guides the class clown toward friendly humor.

The antitoxin adult in Jay Leno's early life was his father. Jay's dad was a very funny guy who was often asked to get up and speak at conventions. He worked as an insurance salesman in tough Spanish Harlem in New York. He was able to handle challenging situations with his good humor, coupled with his respect for people. His hatred of any form of prejudice, coupled with his love of laughter, provided a powerful model for his son.

SIGNATURE TENDENCIES OF CLASS CLOWNS

Class clowns have certain tendencies in common. All share an almost indefinable talent for inviting people to laugh. There is something magic about them that causes people to respond in a certain way. This something transcends subject matter and seems to relate to an attitude that clowns have toward themselves, others, and the world. This attitude is reflected in a whimsical, nutty, upside-down approach to life that appeals to most people. As one teacher commented, "When you're with a funny student, you become more funny than you are."

A close friend, Don Russell, described the unique popularity of one class clown. In his book *The Chalkdust Trail* (2003), Don describes Jean, the high school class beauty, who was adored and marveled at by every high school boy. Her natural beauty and pleasing manner were greatly admired by everyone. Don wrote:

> Strange as it may seem, Jean attended a large percentage of the dances with Archie Small, the high school class clown. Jean always seemed to be at her best and most beautiful in Archie's presence. Archie was long and lean. He was about two thirds leg, and the rest of him eased up to a rather small head covered like a pineapple with a quarter inch of blond

fuzz. His bright blue eyes and his mischievous grin immediately promoted smiles on the faces of all he met.

Many times I've seen Archie put on a pantomime behind Jean's back which could make any observer ache with laughter. He'd make believe that he was clasping her to his chest, stroke her long hair, and then sweep her off her feet à la Prince Charming. I once asked Archie how he worked his charm on Jean. His response was a sly wink with one bright blue eye and a low "woof, woof." (p. 61)

Martin Seligman, in his book *Authentic Happiness* (2002), describes signature strengths. In our class clown research, Dr. Damico and I were able to identify four class clown signature strengths that separate clowns from nonclowns. We named these investing, asserting, relating, and coping.

Investing represents a trust in one's potential, coupled with an attitude of excitement and wonder. Class clowns are willing to jump in, take risks, and try new things. By investing, class clowns enjoy a release of emotional tension. As Steve Allen explained in a television interview, "In general, I think every comedian knows that you're only one inch away from disaster all the time." Clowns are willing to take bold risks to live life fully.

Asserting is the desire to have as much control as possible over the environment. It is the habit of declaring often and forcefully the existence of personal rights. Class clowns are constantly involved in the process of affirmation to claim their own integrity. When class clowns are treated badly, they either fight back sharply or gather themselves up and seek a more inviting environment. Too often this means dropping out of school.

Relating is the talent of identifying with others and their feelings. It is the ability to establish connections and relationships with fellow human beings. Relating seems to reflect a basic liking of people and a concern for their welfare. As mentioned earlier, class clowns are not usually part of the "in crowd." Their sometimes satirical humor and natural, spontaneous approach to life often make them loners in school.

Coping is the ability to handle difficult situations and overcome obstacles. It is the talent for surviving and usually prevailing. One way or another, class clowns find ways to successfully cope with life's challenges.

The four tendencies serve as the basis for the next four chapters. Together, the signature tendencies are an invitation to relate to others and to ourselves in healthy ways, to assert ourselves when the need arises, and to invest deeply in what life has to offer. These qualities are an open invitation to cope, if not successfully then at least differently from more sober folk.

Some of the following suggestions for channeling the clown's energy and humor into worthwhile classroom endeavors appeared in an earlier book, *Inviting School Success*, which I coauthored with John Novak (Purkey & Novak, 1996). Many suggestions work well with both clowns and nonclowns. However, the following suggestions are designed specifically to cash in on the relatively unique tendencies (investing, asserting, relating, and coping) of class clowns. These four signature tendencies offer important clues on how to work successfully with a special group of talented students. They also provide suggestions on what class clowns can teach us about living, learning, and laughter.

ENCORE

(A REAPPEARANCE AND ADDITIONAL PERFORMANCE)

1. Have Fun. Humor is a wonderful teaching strategy. It teaches concepts and stimulates intellectual development. Moreover, having fun has value in its own right. It need not be justified solely with its positive connections with academic achievement.

Suggestion: Make a list of ways that you have fun and check the list regularly. Enjoying physical activities, reading good books, meeting with close friends, spending time with loved ones, traveling to exciting places are all ways to invite fun and laughter into your life. Make sure you're not shortchanging yourself.

2. Channel Humor. If not properly channeled, humor can become a disruptive force. The teachers' ability to monitor and control the classroom social environment is a hallmark of good teaching.

Suggestion: Follow seven important teacher practices: dress better than your students, provide successful experiences for everyone, plan lessons well ahead, keep your cool, be consistent, be fair, and be professional.

3. Inspirit Your School. Schools can become more welcoming, lighthearted, and enjoyable for everyone. Class clowns help banish boredom, fight monotony, and spread sunshine.

Suggestion: Talk with colleagues about having the first five minutes of every school meeting devoted to "happy talk." Share successes, tell funny stories, sing a humorous school song, or do a skit. Invite everyone to lighten up.

Investing

If only the best singers dared sing, how quiet our world would be

If only the best writers dared write, how ignorant our world would be

If only the best dancers dared dance, how sad our world would be

If only the best athletes engaged in athletics, how weak our world would be

And if only the best lovers made love, where would I be?

(I would be tired.)

—WWP

Investing is the first of four signature tendencies of class clowns. Investing implies a basic confidence in one's potential, regardless of circumstances. For class clowns, investing is a willingness to spend one's psychological capital with the purpose of getting a profitable future benefit. This benefit transcends personal profit. Investing is expending personal capital for a more decent, caring, fun-filled, lighthearted world. Lily Tomlin, world-class comedienne, wrote that as a young girl she loved for people to create something out of nothing, just by using their voice and body.

My colleague and dear friend John Novak, who was, is, and always will be a class clown, shared an episode that happened to him in elementary school. His first-grade teacher became irritated with John and his many questions. Finally, the teacher said, "Johnny, if you think you can do a better job of teaching, come to the front of the class." John thought it was a serious invitation, so he marched to the front of the classroom and began teaching.

Clowns live to take direct action, even at the risk of failure or ridicule. Dan Vicko, a sixth-grade teacher in Livonia, Michigan, shared this episode:

In my first year as a teacher, I had a class clown who thought he would be clever and see if his head could fit through the hole of his chair. He tried it. It worked. However, he couldn't get his head back out of the chair. Staff members and myself couldn't get his head back out. Finally, we had to lather up his head with lotion to free him from the chair. Let's just say he won't be trying that stunt in the near future.

The French phrase, *e'lan' vital* captures the class clown's approach to life: "Vital ardor, glow or burst." Investing means taking risks to live life well.

THE VALUE OF INVESTING

A personal story illustrates the value of investing. Years ago, I was teaching at the University of Florida in Gainesville. One spring day, an announcement appeared in the *Alligator*, the student newspaper. It stated that there would be a Great Bicycle Race sponsored by the Fellowship of Christian Athletes. The bicycle race was to start in Gainesville and end in Cedar Key, a distance of more than fifty miles. All intercollegiate student athletes at the University of Florida were invited to be in the race. Sponsors would be asked to contribute a dollar to the Cancer Crusade for each mile an athlete traveled.

When I read the announcement, I knew I had to enter the race. Although I was a terrible football, baseball, tennis, basketball, and whatever player (too small, too light, too fearful), I was hell on bicycle wheels. Long before cycling became a popular adult sport, I was riding my bike to and from the university. As I thought about the race, I could see myself flying down the highway to Cedar Key and crossing the finish line, flames shooting from the bike's sprockets, popping the drag chute to slow down. I said to myself, "I own this race."

My biggest challenge in entering the race was to obtain a sponsor. At that time, I as teaching a small, intimate seminar of 325 undergraduates. I went to my students and explained that I was entering the Great Bicycle Race and needed their sponsorship. I asked my students to sponsor me. They thought my entry was laughable. What chance would a tired, worn-out, university professor have against the best athletes at the university?

It was at this point that I learned a valuable lesson: If I believe something with all my heart, and if I have the courage to invest in it, and the bravery to share it, the belief will become contagious. Few things are as contagious and powerful as a passionate belief that is acted on.

At the next class meeting, my students approached me and said that everyone in the class was talking about me and my decision to compete against the best athletes at the university. My students had formed a booster group. They would support me like no professor had ever been supported before. Some students took up a collection and received enough money to rent a twenty-four-foot moving truck. A second group of students went to the University of Florida Drama Department and borrowed a beautiful princess-style evening dress of purest silk. Another group obtained a diamond-studded tiara. Yet another group obtained a sterling silver tray, a golden goblet, and a bottle of French champagne. The University of Florida homecoming queen was approached and agreed to help. She would wear the beautiful dress and the sparkling diamond-studded tiara and carry the silver tray.

To top things off, my students lined up the entire University of Florida cheerleading squad. The cheerleaders would ride in the back of the truck and cheer me on to victory.

The plan was for the rental truck to carry the cheerleaders and the homecoming queen. The truck would lead me down the highway to Cedar Key. According to the plan, every ten miles, the truck would stop. The cheerleaders were to jump out and wave their pom-poms. The homecoming queen would stand by the road and hold high the silver tray and golden goblet. My task was to race to the truck, do a wheelie, take one sip of the champagne, and then continue in the race. (It's not who comes in first, it's how you make the trip.)

Twenty-four hours before the Great Bicycle Race I received a call from the president of the Fellowship of Christian Athletes at the University of Florida. He informed me that my application to enter the race had been received and that it had not been approved. He apologized and explained that the race was limited to student athletes. I argued my case, pointing out that I was an athlete (beanbag-toss champion in second grade), to no avail. I was not allowed to enter the race.

At the following class meeting, I informed my students that I had been scratched from the race. The stunned students sat in silence. Suddenly, a student stood up and declared, "Be not dismayed, Dr. Purkey. We'll have our own race! We'll call ourselves "The League of Pagan Slobs!"

And so it happened that one fine spring day more than three hundred of us met and held our own bicycle race to Cedar Key. We had a glorious time, and if you have to ask who won, you don't know enough about winning.

Class clowns exhibit a willingness to invest themselves fully in what life offers. They follow paths even though they don't know where the paths lead. They make promises that they may not be able to keep. Steve Allen, in his book *More Funny People* (1982), wrote that he delighted in giving Mel Brooks an almost impossible topic during their parties. He confided that he always tried to select something that would force Mel into a panic because, according to Allen, a clown's creative mind in panic is a marvelous thing to see. By investing, clowns enjoy a natural high of emotional excitement.

How to Teach Class
Clowns Through Investing

Sharing a classroom with one or more class clowns can be a teacher's worst nightmare. On the other hand, it can be a splendid opportunity to capitalize on the delightful energy, vitality, and intelligence of some very special and often endearing students.

Words of caution are necessary before presenting some successful ways to teach class clowns. Class clowns will never be fully domesticated. No matter what techniques, methods, skills, or knowledge teachers may possess, class clowns will always find a way to jump the fence. While clowns are quick to invest themselves in things they like, they are equally quick to assert themselves and resist the things they don't like. The best the teacher can hope for is to channel the class clowns' special tendency to invest themselves in worthwhile school endeavors.

A second word of caution is for teachers to maintain composure. If a class clown can anger the teacher enough so that the teacher loses composure, then the student controls the teacher. The amateur is ruled by adrenaline, whereas the professional uses it. If the teacher loses control and says the first thing that pops into mind, the teacher will probably give the greatest speech he or she will ever regret. The secret is to slow the pace to avoid emotional escalation, handle one concern at a time, and always consider compromise.

A final word of caution is to keep your sense of humor. Don't be afraid to laugh at funny happenings in the classroom, even though you may be the "goat." Schools and classrooms can be hilarious places. Teachers and students may notice the humor in something being studied, and educators often say funny things they may not have intended to say. To illustrate, here are some

actual public address announcements sent from principals' offices to students and school staff:

The children will please pass out quietly for the
assembly.

All students P through U please go to the yearbook
room.

Will the custodian please go to the bathroom next to
the principal's office?

Someone has been leaving classroom windows open.
You know who you are.

Teachers may leave at the dismissal bell, but please
don't trample the students.

Custodians will not clean rooms 46 and 218 until the
desks are in line.

Will the varsity cheerleaders please come by the principal's office and pick up their skirts?

All those boys with super balls report to the principal's office. (Bouncing "super balls" off the hallway
walls was a student fad.)

Laughter warms a classroom. For example, when a
teacher asks the students to name the youngest and oldest thing in the classroom, the teacher will quickly be
identified by students as the oldest thing. (Be fore-
warned of the laughter sure to come.) However, beyond
the laughter, the search for the oldest and youngest thing
in the classroom opens up all sorts of possibilities to
explore and teach the natural sciences.

Teachers can usually count on class clowns to invest
themselves. Clowns want to have an important role in
making life happen. Diane Jones, a kindergarten teacher,
shared a delightful story of a student investing himself.

At the beginning of the school year, she was standing by her classroom door welcoming the new students when Johnny, a bright-eyed kindergartner, asked the teacher which seat he should take. She motioned to her classroom and replied, "Just go on in and take any seat you like." Several minutes later, she entered the classroom and found Jimmy comfortably settled in the teacher's chair located behind her desk. He had his pencils, paper, and lunchbox neatly laid out and was ready for his first day of school.

The following sections explain some practical strategies that illustrate how teachers can take advantage of class clowns' tendencies to invest themselves in things that interest them.

Share Responsibilities

Successful teachers of class clowns are good managers. They seldom do things that students could do just as well. There are countless ways that teachers can involve clowns constructively in classroom duties. Setting up and operating audiovisual equipment, distributing and collecting materials, arranging and rearranging furniture, tidying up the classroom, and assisting fellow students who are physically challenged are just a few examples of the many ways teachers can encourage class clowns to invest themselves in the educative process.

Another aspect of responsibility is to be accountable for one's actions. Clowns and nonclowns should be required to pay for damaged or lost materials. If students make a mess, they should be required to clean it up. The same is true for inappropriate or uncaring behavior. When a class clown does not know when to quit pushing limits, the teacher can make direct eye contact, move closer, and signal by hand movements.

Sometimes, enough is enough. Excuses do not free us of responsibilities.

One teacher shared a story describing how she encouraged a young class clown, "Roger the Dodger," to invest in a worthwhile classroom activity. This teacher enjoyed having living plants in her classroom. One day, a parent brought her a beautiful green fern, which she placed in a bright sunlit corner of the classroom. Roger the Dodger said to his teacher, "It is obvious that you don't know nothing about ferns. They like shade." The teacher promptly named Roger the Dodger the Royal Protector of Classroom Plants. His special assignment was to care for all of the classroom plants. He accepted the assignment with great pride. He even had a cardboard crown that he wore whenever he tended to his plants. The plants did beautifully the rest of the school year—and so did Roger the Dodger, the Plant Manager.

Another way to invest clowns is to obtain a hardy little animal and create an environmentally comfortable world for it. For example, a turtle or lizard needs a large aquarium with a warm rock for sunbathing and a little pool for swimming. One classroom had an iguana with its own ladder, which allowed the iguana to climb onto the windowsill to enjoy the view and sunshine. Of course, teachers need to supervise clowns in the proper care of the class pet (particularly when the pet is a reptile).

Form Triads

A valuable way to encourage class clowns to invest themselves in worthwhile classroom learning is to form student triads. Each triad consists of three students. The triads are provided with sufficient classroom time to conduct research on an assigned topic. Each triad is asked to research their topic to obtain information, prepare materials, and teach a minilesson to the entire class. The minilesson should be on a topic that fits with the classroom academic curriculum.

Placing a class clown with two serious-minded classmates allows the clown to use his or her creative skills in socially acceptable ways. (In India, elephant trainers place untrained elephants between two well-trained ones to teach the untrained elephant how to behave.) When triad members know that each triad is required to present its work to the entire class, the triad members tend to stay on task and focus on the work at hand.

Spotlight Talent

A great way to satisfy the class clown's desire to show off is to arrange a showcase for his or her abilities. Look for ways to provide opportunities for a schoolwide display of talents. Class clowns are talented when it comes to reading a funny story, singing a silly song, doing a stand-up comic routine, mimicking a well-known person (educators beware!), and planning and presenting skits.

Student talent assemblies give class clowns the chance to strut their stuff. All sorts of talents can be showcased, including musical groups, dance acts, readings, tumbling, monologues, juggling, skits, and other entertainment. Class clowns do particularly well with skits. Parents, community members, and groups of older adults in residential care provide an appreciative audience for budding talents.

Another way to spotlight class clowns is to give them the opportunity to serve as student announcers using the school's public address (PA) system. Whether it is to lead the Pledge of Allegiance, offer morning news, or make announcements, class clowns can serve as announcers. They can also present a riddle or quiz of the day.

While usually dependable with this responsibility, clowns have been known to kick over the traces. When one class clown sneezed while making the morning announcements over the school's PA system, he quickly explained to the entire school, "Sorry folks. I just ate a fly." The school was filled with laughter the entire day.

Jack Schmidt, a colleague and friend, said that as a student he was the morning homeroom announcer. Each day, the first announcement called students by name to report to Mr. Follansbee's office, the assistant principal in charge of discipline. Jack decided to break the monotony. On St. Patrick's Day, he began the broadcast with "Happy St. Patrick's Day." Then he continued, "Will the following students please report to Mr. O'Follansbee's office immediately: Donald O'Smith, Rebecca O'Cox, John O'Waters, Nicki O'Bolagno," and so forth. Class clowns have a hard time letting well enough alone.

Many clowns enjoy being the announcer for the school radio or television station. A memorable illustration of a class clown serving as a radio announcer was the performance of Robin Williams in the film *Good Morning, Vietnam.* With a bit of supervised coaching, clowns can do a great job of working in the mass media.

Class clowns have a creative flair for photography and video productions. A school or class videotape can be used for many purposes. For example, a video can inform parents and other visitors about the school, orient new students, and provide information to families who are considering relocation. Videotapes can also be used as part of a video exchange with schools in other parts of the world.

Modify the Grading System

There is no guarantee that successful experiences in school will encourage class clowns to behave appropriately, but they increase the probability that such will take place. On the other hand, unsuccessful experiences practically guarantee disruptive behavior.

Grading systems can be altered to recognize and reward the tendency of class clowns to invest themselves in things of interest. Howard Gardner (1999), Harvard professor and authority on learning styles, introduced the theory of multiple intelligences. He identified more than eight different learning styles. Being creative, composing songs, creating dances, telling stories, drawing images, volunteering for class activities, and thinking in fresh and innovative ways should be rewarded.

Topsy-turvy thinking has resulted in countless inventions and innovations. The person who thought to put the eye of the needle in the nose rather than the tail made the modern sewing machine possible. Great discoveries are often the result of recognizing what others have seen but have not grasped. A classic example is worthy of being presented here.

In 1904, a French scientist accidentally dropped a bottle, which fell on the concrete floor. The bottle shattered, but to the scientist's amazement, the bottle retained its shape. The shattered glass was not scattered about the floor. The scientist recalled that he had used a collodion solution in this particular bottle. The solvent had evaporated, but it left a thin film of cellulose nitrate on the inside of the bottle. Several days later, the scientist learned of an auto accident in which a young person had been cut terribly by flying glass. The scientist connected the two seemingly unrelated events in his mind, and laminated safety glass was the result.

Encourage clowns to put things together so that they make a new kind of sense. For example, you might ask, "What if everyone had twenty fingers, or one finger, or no fingers?" or "What if the earth were shaped like an egg?" Assignments that encourage creative thinking include, for example, to invent a game the world has never seen or to draw a four-sided triangle. The clown's tendency to think in a topsy-turvy, loopy manner is a special talent. This talent has great potential to enrich any classroom.

The grading system might also encourage student self-evaluations. Credit can be given for completing independent study units. Special projects can be evaluated by asking three basic questions. What do you like about your project? What could you do to make it better? How might you do this?

A little spice can be added to tests by giving students a choice of questions (e.g., "Answer nine of the following twelve questions," "Write a question that you wish were on the test and then answer it"). This gives clowns the opportunity to highlight an aspect of the lesson or course that they enjoyed and may have studied.

A good way to encourage clowns' tendency to invest is to invite them to make comments on "objective" tests. On objective tests, such as multiple choice, fill in the blank, and true or false, leave sufficient room following each item for clowns to make comments regarding their answers. Sometimes the answers are perfectly acceptable when the teacher understands the context in which the answers are given. For example, I once asked my eighth-grade students to describe how air and water are alike. My resident class clown responded, "They're both fluid." He explained his answer by saying, "They both flow"—a perfectly reasonable answer when taken in context.

By asking questions that require more than fill-in-the-blank, multiple-choice, true-false responses, teachers can invite discussion and dialogue. Some questions posed by the teacher may not even have an answer. Zen masters use a special kind of question to invite their students to reflect deeply about themselves and their relationship with the world. They use a koan. A koan is a simple question that has no simple answer (e.g., "How would you describe beauty?" "What happens when an irresistible force hits an immovable object?" or "Can God create a boulder so large that He cannot move it?"). It is the student's struggle with the koan, rather than the teaching of the master, that enlightens the student. The same is true for ironic questions (e.g., "Is there pleasure in pain?" "Why do bad things happen to good people?" "Do ends justify the means?"). The class clowns' keen intelligence, rich imagination, and sharp wit will add fun and laughter to the discussion.

Encourage Special Interest Groups

Form student special interest groups (SIGs). The possibilities for in-school clubs are endless. Sponsors can be found for chess clubs, hiking clubs, nature clubs, academic clubs, audiovisual clubs, science clubs, investor clubs, astronomer clubs, jogging clubs, math clubs, acting clubs, music clubs, magician clubs, debate clubs, and comic clubs. There are countless other school clubs.

A club that usually has great appeal to class clowns is a collector's club. Collections can range from stamps and coins to baseball cards and toys. The purpose of introducing a collector's club is to take advantage of the class clowns' tendency to invest in matters of interest. Encourage clowns to begin collections. If they already have a collection, invite them to display it in the school. If they don't have a collection, work to get them started. Collecting can lead to all sorts of investing opportunities. In some cases, investing in collections leads to exciting careers. Collecting will stimulate clowns' creativity. When clowns are stimulated creatively, they become engaged in the learning process.

What Class Clowns Can Teach Us About Investing

Lynn Johnston (1994), creator of the popular cartoon series *For Better or For Worse,* wrote that as a child she loved to draw pictures. If they got her into trouble, it was worth it. If it succeeded in making people laugh, she was "high." The message here is to invest yourself in getting as much joy out of life as you can without being cruel or toxic. If teachers are not going to be paid a respectable wage, they should at least enjoy themselves.

Class clowns are investment gamblers, constantly risking everything for a laugh. They do what they believe is funny: win, lose, place, show, or draw. A classic example of the class clown mentality is that of Mel Brooks, comic actor and creator of the Broadway smash hit *The Producers.* He is known for his brilliantly zany willingness to jump off comedic ledges. He either soars like an eagle or drops like a stone.

This brings us to three pieces of advice that class clowns might offer teachers: (1) Any attempt is a victory; (2) if it's worth doing, it's worth doing poorly; and (3) be a rubber ball.

Any Attempt Is a Victory

For class clowns, the question is, "Did I try and fail, or did I fail to try?" There is an adage in basketball that you miss one hundred percent of the shots you don't take. The victory is in the attempt. For class clowns, life is not a spectator sport. It is a full-contact participant sport.

In junior high school, I played center on the football team. I could snap the ball effectively. My problem was that I weighed 120 pounds. Do you know how much playing time is allocated to a 120-pound, third-string, ticklish center? But at least I tried. I had something to talk about in the locker room.

Clowns are often the first to volunteer, even if it places them in the path of defeat. Any investment in living, no matter how small or in what area, has tremendous potential. The smallest action can be more significant than the largest intention. Comedienne Cynthia Heimel even went so far as to give this advice: "When in doubt, make a fool of yourself. There is a microscopically thin line between being brilliantly creative and acting like the most gigantic idiot on earth. So what the hell, leap!"

A very funny friend, Eddie Collins, told me that if we wait until everything is ready, we've waited too long. He taught me the importance of deciding what I want and then going for it. Eddie's advice to me was to take paths that lead to unknown places, give promises that I may not be able to keep, and eat foods that I have never before tasted. As an example, Eddie used a scene from the film *Gone with the Wind.* Ben, the freed slave, is leaving the plantation, Tara. Scarlett O'Hara asks him where he is going. He replies, "I don't know, Miss Scarlett, but I'm on freedom road." It is important to make the effort. If we wait until we have time to make the effort, what happens when our time is up?

I once had the pleasure dining with a young athlete who had been a member of a recent United States Olympic team. She had not won any medals. During our meal, she made a comment worth repeating here. She said, "Taking part is winning, not taking part is losing, and that is what winning and losing are all about."

Making the attempt is half the battle, but it is what many people fear most. Every time I pass a graveyard, I think of the dreams that are buried there. I reflect on all those who might have been dancers, all those who might have been singers or poets or artists. They lacked the courage to try. They sleep in a garden of dead dreams.

I cannot speak for others, but when I die I want to have used up all of my tickets. I don't want to find myself standing in some cosmic parking lot, holding up some unused tickets and shouting, "Anybody want free tickets? I don't want money for them. I just hate seeing them go to waste." Clowns remind us that life loves the person who has the courage to invest in it fully. Will Rogers said it best: "Don't be afraid of your mind. It will lead you to humor."

If It's Worth Doing, It's Worth Doing Poorly

The value of imperfection is reflected in Homer's *Odyssey*. In this monumental epic, Ulysses meets Calypso, who is immortal. She is fascinated by Ulysses and envies him because he will not live forever. His life somehow becomes more vibrant, fuller; every decision is more significant because his time on earth is limited. What he chooses to do represents real choice and real risk.

If there is no chance of failure, then success is meaningless. If there is no chance of death, life is meaningless. What makes life so exciting is that it is so imperfect and unpredictable. It will never come again.

The greatest mistake you can make in life is to continually fear that you'll make one. Hugh Prather, a minister and author, expressed this idea beautifully: "I sometimes react to making a mistake as if I have betrayed myself. My fear of making a mistake seems to be based on the hidden assumption that I am potentially perfect and that if I can just be very careful I will not fall from heaven." The irrational passion for perfection takes all the joy out of life.

You can be very good at things that you are not good at, but the price you pay is great. Surely, there are few things in life as sad as the person who has committed his or her life to being perfect in every way, even at the expense of everything else he or she holds dear. The 2004 Hollywood film *The Stepford Wives* illustrates the danger of being overly committed to perfection. In the film, the Stepford wives are compelled to live up to impossible standards of beauty and attractiveness. The film is a cautionary story about utopian standards that are doomed to fail.

From a class clown's perspective, if people only did the things they can do well, the silence would be deafening. By taking a chance and getting started, even if the start is very poor, people begin their journey toward improvement. Doing things well is what comes from doing things poorly. Slogans such as "Too much analysis leads to paralysis" and "Too much rigor leads to rigor mortis" may be true. Any attempt, no matter how small, is a victory. It brings people closer to their goals.

As this book is written, there are numerous reality shows on television. Contestants submit themselves to surgically augmented breasts, reshaped noses, liposuctioned thighs, enhanced lips, lifted eyebrows, extended hair, capped or veneered teeth, surgically reduced toe size, and other procedures too delicate to mention. Some contestants take muscle-enhancing and often dangerous drugs in an attempt to develop a perfect body.

Even among American children, the search for perfection has resulted in some bizarre practices. Some parents give their children gift certificates for breast enlargements and other plastic surgery. Many teenagers are becoming bulimic and enduring other unhealthy practices to become or stay beautiful. All of these efforts are the result of the endless quest for perfection. It may be possible to reach the pinnacle of perfection, but the rarified air at this high altitude would probably kill people.

Charles Swindell (1983) describes the person who strives to do everything perfectly as the over-expecter.

For the over-expecter, enough is never enough. The over-expecter sends the message that no matter how hard you try, you have not measured up. Furthermore, you never will. He writes, "Fun fades, laughter leaves, and what remains? This won't surprise anybody: the tyranny of the urgent, the uptight, the expected, always the expected, which, being interpreted, means, the making of a coronary" (p. 224). The over-expecter is constantly haunted by his or her imperfections. It is not surprising that there are countless people who avoid achievement situations simply because they cannot be perfect in their efforts.

The value of imperfection was underscored by Gerald W. Johnson (1934), who declared that our society needs more bum music because attaining good music these days is not an achievement.

We are rapidly becoming a generation of voyeurs, peeking through the cracks of life. There are few of us today who don't own tape recorders, record players, VCRs, CDs, computerized music, several television sets, two or three radios. But when was the last time you've been with friends crowded around a piano, singing poorly at the top of your lungs?

We crowd into stadiums on a weekend, eighty thousand strong, to watch twenty-two superbly conditioned athletes running up and down the field getting exercise they don't need. We let Peyton Manning play our game. We allow Britney Spears to dance our dance. We permit Natalie Cole to sing our song. We let Lance Armstrong ride our bicycle. We sit, watch, and listen to the people who can do things well.

How tragic it is to be so afraid of imperfection that we dare not risk being human. This fear inhibits human potential. The distance from doing things poorly to doing things well is only a step. The distance between not doing things and doing things poorly is infinite.

Forget about perfection, which Hugh Prather called slow death. Class clowns invite us to give our dreams an honest shot.

Be a Rubber Ball

Glass balls shatter when dropped on a hard surface. Rubber balls bounce. Work to be flexible under stress. Seek ways to bounce without breaking. See challenges as opportunities rather than problems. Consider mistakes as lessons, embarrassing moments as funny.

One teacher described a little class clown who thought it was funny to disappear. As the teacher brought her class in from recess, she thought she saw the clown dart into the boys' restroom. The teacher marched halfway into the restroom and shouted, "All right, young man, you come out of there!" At that moment, she glanced down and recognized the principal's shoes under one of the restroom stalls. Later, she and the principal had a big laugh over the embarrassing moment.

A good way to be a rubber ball is to redirect rather than confront. Find alternatives to power struggles. It is sometimes wise to admit ignorance, especially when working with class clowns. Instead of struggling to know everything, take time to say, "I don't know, but I'll find out." Follow this up with, "What do you think?" Class clowns will be impressed with the your honesty. They will also be pleased that you asked for their opinions. Don't be afraid to admit that on some days a clown might be the best teacher in the classroom.

One final tip on how to be a rubber ball comes from scuba diving. Many authorities encourage teachers to take "a deep breath" to reduce tension. Scuba divers offer a better approach. They exhale all bad air before inhaling. The next time a class clown or anyone else is getting on your nerves, slowly exhale all of the stale air from your lungs and follow this with a gradual deep breath. It reduces tensions almost immediately.

Investing is what class clowns do best. This chapter discussed the importance of investing and explained how the clown's tendency to invest can be a valuable asset in the classroom. The chapter concluded with some suggestions from class clowns on how teachers might invest themselves more fully in life. Chapter 4 considers a second signature characteristic of class clowns: the tendency to assert themselves.

ENCORE

(A REAPPEARANCE AND ADDITIONAL PERFORMANCE)

1. Teach to Pass. There is growing research evidence that failure begets failure. Failing one subject today correlates with failing more subjects tomorrow.

Suggestion: Declare war on failure. Don't tolerate it. Under a strong teacher there are no weak students.

2. Practice Good Management. Successful teachers are good managers. They share classroom responsibilities to encourage students to invest themselves in the educative process.

Suggestion: Delegate duties by assigning students to set up and take down equipment, handle lights, align desks, empty trashcans, distribute and collect materials, and handle other classroom chores.

3. Use Small-Group Activities. Small groups allow class clowns to talk and move around. Small groups encourage students to further invest themselves in learning.

Suggestion: Divide the class into small film companies. Each company is to prepare a two-minute commercial on an academic concept. Each company is expected to write, direct, and videotape its commercial for class viewing.

Asserting

I've always followed my father's advice: He
told me . . . never insult anybody unintentionally. If I insult you, you can be goddamn sure I
intend to.

—John Wayne in *Quotable
Hollywood* (Sullivan, 2001)

Asserting is the second signature tendency of class clowns. Asserting may be defined as the ability to establish and fight for one's dignity and self-respect. It reflects confidence in one's own value, abilities, and self-directing powers. Class clowns do not hesitate to exercise their own self-directing powers. Clowns are aware that they have some control over what happens to them.

Class clowns assert themselves by challenging authority and maintaining a voice in what is taking place. They are quick to step forward and claim their rights. They speak up for their own ideas, and they do not hesitate to stand up to authority. For example, I observed an elementary school class clown say to a teacher, "You shouldn't talk to Billy so mean." Friendly clowns understand that feelings are important and deserve respect.

THE VALUE OF ASSERTING

Innovations and improvements in any organization are rarely made unless people are willing to stand up, step forward, ask questions, and assert their rights.

Asserting is the ability to take action that enables people to act in their own best interests, to stand up for themselves without undue anxiety, to express their honest feelings comfortably, and to exercise their own rights without denying the rights of others. Beyond affirming one's own rights, assertive behavior involves the ability to express feelings of positive regard and appreciation.

Herb Gardner (1962) captured the value of asserting in his book *A Thousand Clowns:*

> I want him to know exactly the special thing he is or else he won't notice it when it starts to go. I want him to stay awake and know who the phonies are. I want

him to know how to holler and put up an argument. I want a little guts to show before I can let him go. I want to be sure he sees all the wild possibilities. I want him to know it's worth all the trouble just to give the world a little goosing when you get the chance. And I want him to know the subtle, sneaky, important reason why he was born a human being and not a chair. (p. 70)

It was probably a class clown who announced to one and all that the king had no clothes on! My recent experience with a tiny class clown illustrates how clowns assert themselves.

I am an educational consultant, which means I spend a lot of time in schools. Often when I enter an elementary classroom, the teacher introduces me to the students like so: "Class, this is Dr. Purkey." The students have been taught to respond in unison, "Good morning, Dr. Purkey." In one classroom, when the teacher introduced me, all of the students gave me the usual greeting, except one little boy. When I was introduced, he jumped out of his chair, marched up to me, introduced himself, and shook my hand. The teacher was embarrassed with the child's assertive behavior, but all I could see was a delightful little class clown.

The great comedian Jack Benny was considered to be the most assertive comedian to ever stand on a stage. He was a master of simply standing on the stage, looking bemused, saying absolutely nothing, and waiting an eternity for what he wanted. Practicing wait time is an excellent teaching strategy for maintaining good classroom behavior. Benny asserted himself through his courage to wait as well as his sense of humor.

An unforgettable example of a class clown recklessly asserting himself is the classic scene in the film *Mr. Roberts.* A young naval officer, played by Jack Lemmon, barges into the despotic captain's office and declares, "Captain, it is I, Ensign Pulver, and I want you to know that I just threw your stinkin' palm tree overboard. Now what's all this crud about no movie tonight?" A clown's intellect on the offensive can be fearsome.

How to Teach Class Clowns Through Asserting

As mentioned earlier, class clowns are quick to assert themselves. Attempting to bottle up a clown's tendency to assert is like trying to bottle up a hurricane. When encountering resistance from a class clown, it is usually wise to be flexible. Always consider compromise when challenged. When faced with resistance, think of alternatives. In other words, never enter a room without exits. The teacher who sends a misbehaving student to the principal's office with the public declaration, "You're out and you're never coming back to this classroom!" will probably end up eating his or her words. Issuing threats that can't be carried out is dangerous business.

Choosing words carefully is particularly important in working with clowns. One teacher scolded a little class clown by stating, "Young man, you can settle down, or you can go straight home!" When the teacher turned away, the little clown disappeared.

Toody Byrd, a wonderful teacher and counselor, and a super class clown, offered a good example of teacher foot-in-mouth disease. Toody saw herself as the savior of wayward adolescents. In her role as savior, she worked with a high school boy who was the son of a famous rock star. Whenever the father would go away on tour, Billy would skip school. Toody called Billy into her office and gave him an earful. She pointed out the handicaps under which he would be functioning if he did not get a high school diploma. She stressed that he would not be able to get a job or support a family. Then she went for the kill with "You won't even be able to buy a car!" At that very moment, as her words left her mouth, her mind flashed to two cars, parked side by side in the parking lot: Toody's sixteen-year-old, wheezing Pontiac and Billy's brand new Mercedes. Make your words tender because you may have to eat them.

Here are some practical suggestions for using the signature tendency of clowns to assert themselves.

Be Positive With Directives

Some teachers give negative, counterproductive directives: Don't talk, don't run, don't push, don't shove, don't cheat, don't steal, don't interrupt, don't touch, and so on. Such directions would be perfect for a pet rock. Make directions positive by stating what should be done, rather than what should not be done. For example, "don't be late" can be changed to "please arrive on time." Instead of, "don't interrupt," try "please wait your turn." "Don't run" can be changed to "please walk." "Don't yell" can be converted to "speak softly." Class clowns are more likely to conform when directives are positive.

In addition to being positively worded, directives should be brief, clear, and simple. Give precise instructions for desired procedures. Along with clear directives, give reasons why the directives are important. If rules are reasonable, they are far more likely to be obeyed.

One aspect of being positive is to present real options to class clowns. Offer choices that demonstrate respect for the student and communicate a desire for the student to learn from his or her choices. For example, a disruptive class clown might be given the choice of moving to another chair, going to a time-out area, visiting the counselor's office, or staying after school to help the teacher.

The goal of directives is maximum compliance with minimum effort.

Some teachers are guilty of inviting students to events in ways that suggest hope that the invitation will not be accepted, as in the following examples:

You can join the school club *if* you want to.

You are welcome to try out, *but* you need to get here early.

We would love to have you join us. *However,* we are almost full.

It is better to send unconditional invitations, such as simple declarative statements of support: "I want you to try out for the school play. Will you do this for me?" Asking class clowns to do something for the teacher usually works well. For example, in working to improve a clown's behavior, call the student aside and give three positive comments regarding his or her work. Then, quickly follow it up with your wish, as in this example: "Mary, I am pleased with your homework, I like your delightful sense of humor, *and* I wish that you would get to class on time. Will you do this for me?" This is a very mild-mannered way of encouraging desirable student behavior.

Use No-Cut Contracts

Explain to students the long-lasting effects of racist, sexist, homophobic, and other negative comments. Prepare a written no-cut contract, in which everyone agrees to the following classroom rules:

I will not put you down.

You will not put me down.

I will not put myself down.

You will not put yourself down.

Everyone in the classroom, including the teacher, signs the contract. There is a clear understanding by everyone about what each person will do and what each can expect from others. If the teacher or the students break the contract by depreciating themselves or others, they should be gently but firmly reminded of the contract. The contract also curbs the tendency of hostile clowns' assertiveness to take the form of meanness or cruelty.

Reminding class clowns and errant students of the no-cut contract violation is best done in private. Respecting students' feelings by reprimanding in private avoids embarrassing the student. Class clowns are likely to assert themselves inappropriately when they are reprimanded publicly.

Promote Civility

Common courtesy, civility, and politeness are valuable tools when working with all students. These values are encouraged by promoting the words "please" and "thank you." The need for civility is particularly important when working with class clowns. A clown's tendency to assert himself or herself means that the clown will quickly strike back at any real or perceived slight. Avoid trying to control clowns' anger and sarcasm or trying to outwit or be funnier than class clowns. Such attempts, as Burr Snider (2005) pointed out, usually fail.

One way to promote civility is to call students by their preferred names. It is wise to ask students by what name they wish to be called. Some students prefer the short form of their names (e.g., "Bill" rather than "William," "Betty" rather than "Elizabeth."), whereas others don't. Above all, avoid nicknames that embarrass students. One class clown commented, "My last name is Cribbage, and the teacher found it funny to call me 'Mr. Cabbage.' It was a declaration of war."

Ribbings and put-downs are reserved for individuals of equal rank or status who respect each other. For teachers to employ put-downs with students is a misuse of power and authority. It is also risky because class clowns can have a rapid-fire, instantaneous comeback, particularly when they feel that someone is trying to crush their psychological bones.

Another way to encourage politeness is for the teacher to maintain a certain formality with students. Being overly friendly can cause major friction between teachers and students. This is especially important in working with class clowns. Clowns are the most likely of students to test limits with their assertive behavior. Insist that students address all faculty and staff as "Mister, Missus, Miss, Doctor," or other appropriate title. Students are expected to use the last names of all faculty and staff. This expectation should also be maintained when students refer to other professionals in the school, including custodians, nurses, teachers' aides, security officers, and food service personnel.

Burr Snider (2005) suggests the mature class technique. The idea here is to explain to the entire class that you would like to be able to have fun with the class, but you can do this only if the class is mature enough to understand the right time and place for fun and games. The appeal for student maturity is usually effective.

One further way to encourage politeness is to ensure that every directional sign in and around the school begins with "please" and ends with "thank you." Using positively worded signs is one way to improve the atmosphere of the school. For example, "Please walk in hallways" usually works better than "No running in hallways." Every sign should be polite and positively worded. The following list shows some inviting signs and their disinviting counterparts:

Inviting Signs	Disinviting Signs
Please walk on sidewalks.	Keep off grass.
Students are welcome.	No students allowed.
Please use other door.	Keep this door shut.
Visitor parking.	No parking.
Welcome.	No trespassing.
Please eat in designated areas.	No food or drink allowed.

When class clowns are told, "Do not eat the apple!" their usual response is "Where is it?"

Signs posted on and in school buildings can also be humorous. There is a school in London, England, that had a low enrollment of students and was in danger of being closed down. The teachers posted a large sign outside the school that read "All trespassers will be enrolled."

Involve Clowns in Decisions

Whenever possible, involve students in decision making. Students can help make decisions regarding student conduct, academic expectations, school activities, and even textbook reviews. Students can help decide on general classroom rules and penalties for infractions. It's hard for class clowns to argue with self-imposed rules of conduct.

Jim Carrey, the delightful rubber-faced comedian and actor, said that he reached a deal with his junior high school teacher. So long as he did not interrupt the class for a full week, he was allowed to do a ten-minute stand-up comic routine before the class on Friday afternoons.

Involving students also means that ultimatums should be avoided whenever possible. Voluntary and enthusiastic student compliance with rules and regulations is the hallmark of good classroom management. Include everyone who is influenced by a policy to be a part of the policy-making process.

Make sure that classroom policies belong to the entire class. Class clowns are highly sensitive to pretensions and sugarcoated demands. They are quick to assert themselves if they feel they are being conned. Collaboration of students in policy development is an excellent way to encourage class clowns to assert themselves in positive ways. Ownership of rules and regulations is vital. As one wag commented, "No customer washes a rental car."

WHAT CLASS CLOWNS CAN TEACH US ABOUT ASSERTING

The tendency of clowns to assert themselves offers some valuable suggestions for teachers: (1) Keep a sense of humor, (2) don't take yourself too seriously, (3) challenge authority, and (4) promote democratic values.

Keep a Sense of Humor

Keeping a sense of humor is so critical to teaching, learning, and living that it needs to be stated again. A sense of humor is a tonic for healthy living. Henry Ward Beecher called humor "God's medicine." It serves as a wonderful defense against tyranny, a safety valve for adjusting to difficult circumstances, a stimulus for creative enterprise, and the best defense against depression.

Robin Williams said, "I make myself laugh when I'm nude in front of the mirror, pointing out where I've been." Maintaining a sense of humor requires that we are able to laugh at ourselves and at our situations. Some teachers seem to think that they will sprout tails if they dare laugh. In stressful situations, when clowns are busy asserting themselves, the teacher's sense of humor is essential.

A good example of keeping one's sense of humor in a stressful situation was provided by my friend, Claudia Cornett. She told the story of a substitute teacher who experienced the age-old trick in which all of her students dropped their books at the same moment. After they did so, the substitute teacher went to her desk, dropped some books, and said, "Sorry I'm late." Her humorous response broke the ice and turned the situation to her favor. The stunned students were delighted with her humorous response.

A classic example of a sense of humor was provided by the great Italian conductor Arturo Toscanini. During a rehearsal of the New York Symphony Orchestra, Toscanini flew into a tantrum with a player and ordered the musician from the stage. As the musician reached the exit door, he turned and shouted, "Nuts to you!" Yelled back Toscanini, "It's too late to apologize!" Showing a sense of humor can sometimes ease the strain and give people a breather. Humor, when well timed, can be the catalyst that removes tension and resolves concerns. People who take themselves too seriously are probably facing emotional difficulties.

Don't Take Yourself Too Seriously

The clear message from class clowns to educators is to lighten up. Resist the desire to squelch clownish behavior. According to Bertrand Russell, one of the warning signs of an approaching heart attack, stroke, or nervous break-down is the belief that one's work is terribly important. To lighten up is to encourage a cheerful state of mind. Hungarian-born psychologist Mihaly Csikszentmihalyi (pronounced "chik-sent-me-hi") explored the concept of flow, which is the feeling of complete engagement and joy in a creative, playful, fun-filled activity.

A day without laughter is a day without sunshine. Life is short, but there is always room for laughter. Keep looking and you will find something funny, even in the most serious situations. Humor is often found by looking back at experiences that at the time were chaotic. It is only later that we see how the experiences were funny. Humor serves as a shock absorber for past misfortunes and a defense mechanism for future hardships.

Here is a moving example of humor being used as a shield against the finality of death. Stanley Laurel, of *Laurel and Hardy* fame, was lying in his hospital room during his final days. A nurse entered his room to administer emergency assistance. Stan looked up and said, "You know what? I'd a lot rather be skiing." The nurse responded, "Do you ski, Mr. Laurel?" He said, "No, but I'd a lot rather be skiing than doing this."

The need for lightheartedness is clearly evident in the joyless culture found in many public schools. An illus-tration of the need for educators to lighten up was pro-vided by my recent visit to a high school. A student had been expelled because she had dyed her hair bright blue. When I heard about this, I said to the principal, "If you expel everyone in this school with dyed hair, you won't have a teacher left."

I wrote a story, *Miracle at Herbert Hoover High,* that describes how a class clown, Max Coleman, made the highest standardized test scores in the history of Herbert Hoover High School. The story was an effort to invite educators to lighten up.

The story begins with all students at Herbert Hoover High School taking a high-stakes, mandated, standardized achievement test, one of many inflicted on today's students. During the test, all of the students struggled to answer the myriad multiple-choice questions. All, that is, except Max Coleman, resident class clown. He spent his time creating Christmas tree outlines by darkening little bubbles on the answer sheet.

When time was called to end the test, all of the answer sheets were collected, packaged, and mailed to the Educational Testing Service in Princeton, New Jersey. There they were graded using a computerized process that scored, at blinding speed, thousands of answer sheets.

Around midnight, there was a terrible electrical storm over Princeton. A bolt of lightning hit a transformer at the Educational Testing Service. This bolt hit at the exact moment that Herbert Hoover High's student answer sheets were being graded. The bolt of lightning did little damage, except that it hit at the exact microsecond when Max Coleman's paper was flying through the computer. When Herbert Hoover's student test results were downloaded, Max had a perfect score verbal, perfect score math, and perfect score full scale. He had broken the bank at Monte Carlo!

When the test results arrived at Herbert Hoover High School, a mighty shock wave went through the building. Max, the class clown, had earned the highest scores in the history of Herbert Hoover High. Within minutes, the news reached the teachers' lounge (locally known as the Recovery Room). The teacher of Accelerated Honors Senior English, always alert to stay ahead, remarked, "Just as I suspected." On cue, all of the other teachers joined in. They laughed as they shared Max's many witty statements and the hilarious things he had done in their classrooms.

Max suddenly found himself the center of attention. The great "Wizard of Oz" computer had given Max the one thing he didn't have: a Doctor of Thinkology! From that day forward, Max was hailed by all as a great thinker and humorist.

After I shared my story about Max Coleman with a group of educators, a teacher approached me and said, "Dr. Purkey, that's an interesting story about Max Coleman. It proves one thing." I asked, "What is that?" She responded, "We need better computers." I said, "No, we need more electrical storms." I never found out what happened to Max. It is rumored that he is now an award-winning professor at a major university.

Now, whenever the weather reports call for bad weather, and thunderstorms are forming over Princeton, New Jersey, I suspect that another class clown is on his or her way to stardom.

Challenge Authority

There are times when it is necessary to challenge authority. It is always tempting to pop an overinflated ego. Challenging authority with good humor is a powerful weapon against the brute force of oppression.

Clowns assert themselves by challenging unquestioned authority. They possess a built-in "crap detector" that recognizes nonsense, arrogance, and certainty. It was Voltaire who reminded us that doubt is not a very agreeable status, but certainty is a ridiculous one. Clowns are usually the first to become restless when under the thumb of arrogant authorities. They have a low tolerance for boredom or for those who have a proclivity for balderdash.

Class clowns have a special talent for attacking pomposity. There is an almost indefinable power in humor. Satire, mimicry, and ridicule are powerful weapons. Woe be unto those who cross class clowns when the power is on them. The ancient Greeks recognized this power in their myths. Thalia, the muse of comedy, was the child of Zeus, the king of gods. The ancient Greeks defined this comic power as a divine spark, when one transcends everyday life for a brief moment and becomes almost godlike.

The 1948 presidential race is a good example of comic power. The Republican presidential candidate, Thomas Dewey, was ahead in all of the polls. Then it was suggested by some wag that he looked like he had fallen off a wedding cake. Some believe that his presidential campaign never recovered from this satirical observation.

To illustrate the need to challenge authority, there is the urban legend of Herman J. Mankiewicz, one of the all-time best Hollywood humorous writers. Few could match his comic wit, sense of mayhem, or deflationary bards. His encounter with Harry Cohn is one of the most talked-about moments in Hollywood history.

Harry Cohn, head of Columbia Motion Pictures, was an executive bully who delighted in summoning his staff to have lunch with him in his private executive dining room. He would sit at the end of a large table and proceed to bait new employees with barbed insults. When Mankiewicz showed up for lunch, Cohn quickly turned on him with crude and offensive comments. Finally, Cohn, tired of his cruel game, decided to change the subject. Here is how Max Wilk (1973), a film writer who was at the luncheon, described the incident:

Someone mentioned a new film. Cohn had seen it the night before, and it was, in his opinion, rotten. Another Columbia executive tried to argue the point, but Cohn would not hear him out. "The picture stank," he said. "And I know." He had, it seemed, an infallible test of a film's success or failure, and it was his own ass. "If it itches," Cohn proclaimed, "the picture stinks. If it doesn't itch, then the picture's going to be a hit." Silence greeted this ukase, and then Mankiewicz could not stand Cohn's arrogance a moment longer. "I never knew before," he said, "that the entire American motion-picture audience is wired to Harry Cohn's ass." The dining room burst into laughter. Mankiewicz got up, left the dining room, and without needing to be told what to do, he went down to his office, cleaned out his desk, and departed from Columbia Pictures forever. (p. 200)

There are times when class clowns cannot resist sticking pins in pomposity. They can stop a snob, a bully, a pretender, or a pompous ass in his or her tracks. The bigger the balloon, the louder the pop.

Promote Democratic Values

The tendency of class clowns to assert themselves can be channeled into democratic practice. Developing a class constitution requires working together for a common cause. Holding mock elections helps to explain the meaning of democracy. Mock trials can explain the judicial process. Debates on such democratic questions as "Should eighteen-year-olds be eligible to vote?" or "Should the United States reserve the right to invade another country preemptively?" can stir passions. These and other projects are excellent ways to encourage class clowns to assert themselves in positive ways. Best of all, such activities invite class clowns to vigorously dissent from the majority point of view. Vigorous dissent is a hallmark of a democratic society.

A young female class clown demonstrated how to assert herself with composure and dignity. She was sent to the principal's office for the usual infraction, "getting out of line." When the principal began the interview, he asked, "Would you rather that I refer to you as African American or Black?" The girl looked at the principal for a long moment, then replied, "Sir, if it is acceptable to you, I would rather be referred to as 'Jo Anne.'"

Class clowns tend to be polite, but they do not hesitate to assert themselves by challenging authority, particularly when the authority steps on their sense of human dignity. This tendency to assert would certainly be a valuable quality for teachers who often encounter hostile and unfair criticism.

This chapter described the value of assertive behavior. Teachers can use the clowns' tendency to assert themselves by developing clown-friendly teaching methods. The lessons that teachers can learn from the clown's signature tendency to assert is to keep a sense of humor, to challenge authority, and to promote democratic values in the classroom. Chapter 5 introduces a third signature tendency of class clowns, the tendency to relate to others at a personal and significant level.

ENCORE

(A REAPPEARANCE AND ADDITIONAL PERFORMANCE)

1. Be Flexible. A tree without flexibility is easily broken. Palm trees survive hurricanes because they bend without breaking. An important lesson learned from nature is that flexibility is strength, whereas rigidity is weakness.

Suggestion: When working with class clowns, find ways to bend without breaking. When faced with resistance, vary your approach. Seek to redirect unwanted behavior.

2. Be Courteous. The need for politeness is particularly important when working with class clowns. A clown's tendency to assert means that he or she will quickly strike back at discourteous behavior.

Suggestion: Use "please" and "thank you" at every opportunity. Civility and courtesy are critical in developing healthy classroom relationships.

3. Establish Boundaries. Maintain a certain distance from students. Class clowns find it particularly tempting to cross the line and become casual and overfriendly.

Suggestion: Assert yourself when you feel that others are taking advantage of your good nature. Assertive behavior is simply the ability to exercise your own rights and boundaries without denying the rights and boundaries of others.

Relating

I do not teach, I relate.

—Michel de Montaigne

Relating may be defined as connecting with people and the human condition. Because of their tendency to relate, most class clowns are popular with classmates, if not teachers. The clown's upside-down, breezy attitude toward life forms ties between and among individuals. The clown's funny approach to life gives voice to the meaning and purpose of being human.

The class clown's ability to relate to classmates is remarkable. Here is how Mary Lou Frank, a former middle school teacher who is now a professor of psychology at Kennesaw State University, described a funny encounter with a class clown:

> When I began my career, I taught middle school, specifically speech and drama. In my first semester of teaching, I had a student, Ted, who was always up to something (he was helping me learn to be a better teacher). One day, he went in the auditorium before class and hid behind the stage podium. While I was giving the day's lesson and facilitating discussion on the nature of comedy and tragedy, the students couldn't stop laughing. While I was talking, Ted would stick out one leg, or one arm, or both arms, at just the right moment during the class period. It had to be fun to watch.

Life is never so busy that there is no time left for laughter.

The Value of Relating

Human relationships are essential in living a good life. It is hard to imagine anything worse than being totally disconnected from other human beings. Forming connections with other human beings allows us to become part of a larger whole.

My daughter Cynthia shared an experience she had as a teacher of a disconnected little girl whom I will call Bertha. In school, Bertha was an unbelievable discipline problem. If anyone even looked at her, she might go into a tantrum, throw things, and shout obscenities. Bertha was almost totally disconnected from other people. She had been dropped off at an orphanage and never knew her parents. Her family life consisted of a long series of temporary foster homes. Because of her highly aggressive behavior in school, Bertha had no friends.

Cynthia saw Bertha not as a problem but as an opportunity. At every turn, Cynthia would encourage Bertha to relate to other students. Cynthia would take time to talk with Bertha privately and to learn what the world looked like from Bertha's point of view. Cynthia did everything she could to make the classroom a more inviting place for the little girl. However, for most of the school year, Cynthia's efforts met with little success. Bertha continued to throw her tantrums, although not quite as often.

The real measure of Cynthia's success arrived on the last day of school. Bertha brought to class a rumpled red Valentine's box shaped like a heart. At the end of the day, she placed her heart on my daughter's desk and said good-bye. After Bertha left, my daughter lifted the lid and found a note. It read "To the Best Teacher in the World. Signed Bertha." To a student starving for relationships, one teacher can make a profound difference.

HOW TO TEACH CLASS CLOWNS THROUGH RELATING

The ways in which class clowns relate to teachers and classmates seem to correlate with how much they believe that others like and respect them. Teachers who understand the importance of relationships work to remove barriers and encourage togetherness. Some effective ways to remove barriers and encourage healthy interactions are to (1) use inclusive pronouns, (2) brighten the classroom, (3) build class spirit, (4) conduct field studies, and (5) play that funky music.

Use Inclusive Pronouns

Using such pronouns as "we," "us," and "our" is much more likely to create a positive classroom environment than using words such as "you," "yours," and "mine." For example, "We need to finish our work" is more preferable than "You students must complete your work." Most athletic coaches are experts at using inclusive pronouns—for example, "We have to play our best against Central High" or "It is up to us to win this contest." Coaches know that everyone on the team is in the game together.

A specific teacher behavior that invites feelings of belonging in students is the use of "our" statements to suggest membership: *our* curriculum, *our* team, *our* decorations, *our* classroom, *our* rules, *our* classmates, and *our* efforts to keep the school clean.

One valuable way to encourage students to think in terms of "us," "we," and "our" is to share experiences. When done appropriately, show and tell works well with almost any group of students. Ask your students, "Among your personal treasures, what says something about you?" Invite students to bring their mementos to school and tell about them in a sharing session. By talking about their treasures, they are really talking about themselves. Sharing is an effective way to help students get to know each other and to build a feeling of togetherness.

Teachers can join in show and tell by letting students know that they have many dimensions to their life other than that of teacher. Bring a memento to class. Share anecdotes about family, friends, and pets. Tell stories about scary, sad, angry, or funny experiences. One teacher said that she asked her elementary school student if her father was a teacher. The little girl replied, "Oh, no. He works."

Students want to know how you feel about books you have read or films and television programs you have seen. Even moods can be shared. Teachers are often surprised at how caring students can be when they understand that their teacher is having a bad day.

A variation of show and tell is "show and smell." Students bring to class a plastic, sealable bag with something smelly inside. Students can hold a contest to see who can identify the most odors. Needless to say, the teacher will need to closely monitor what clowns bring to class.

Brighten the Classroom

The teacher is the single most important source of brightness in the classroom. Try to begin every class with some good news about what is happening in the school, the local community, and the larger world. Ask students to share their good news. Five minutes of happy talk can set the stage for a super day.

The classroom physical environment is an important factor in brightening classrooms. No matter how attractive, classroom decorations and furniture layout get stale. Even museums change their exhibits regularly. Change the classroom around periodically. A change in layout can result in a change in outlook, both for teachers and students. Fight dreariness and squalor as much as possible. Even lining up the shades, arranging the chairs in an attractive fashion, storing equipment in closets, and keeping the room free of trash can make a big difference in any classroom.

To further brighten the classroom, appoint or elect a student committee to create a monthly or yearly theme.

The theme could be seasonal or based on a special event. A cheerful theme can enrich the classroom. It also impresses visitors when they enter the room.

Sometimes teachers must assert themselves to brighten their classrooms. This includes asking for needed repairs (including a fresh coat of paint, stronger lightbulbs, and new neon lights) and requesting dependable and adequate equipment and supplies. A teacher friend (former class clown) provided a good example of assertiveness. She approached the principal and requested some needed repairs in her classroom. The principal's response was "no." He explained that all repairs would be done during the summer break. One week later, the teacher again approached her principal and requested the repairs. The principal said, "Didn't I tell you 'no'?" To which the teacher responded, "Yes, but that was last week. By now, you may have changed your mind and found a way to have the repairs made now." The repairs were soon made.

Bulletin boards with photos of students, faculty, and staff engaging in out-of-school activities and special interests contribute to the brightness of any classroom. Students can be encouraged to design up-to-date bulletin boards for their classroom and the school's hallways. This is a good way to involve class clowns in the life of the school. It also enhances cooperation and encourages creativity.

Classroom bulletin boards also should be kept up-to-date. It is disconcerting to enter a classroom in March and see on a bulletin board "Welcome to a New School Year."

Perhaps the single most important way to brighten the classroom is for the teacher to pay careful attention to his or her dress. Each day when teachers come to school, they should look like they are going somewhere important. They are not going out to wash the car, mow the lawn, milk the cow, or chop some wood. Teachers do not have to be fashion plates, but they should always dress better than their students.

Build Class Spirit

In self-contained classrooms, teachers can encourage a feeling of togetherness through such simple means as asking the students to select a name for the class. The students might also select a class motto, a class crest logo, and class colors.

Another way to encourage class spirit is to use peer helpers. Peer tutoring works well for students who are having difficulty with certain subjects. It is also a morale booster for students who are providing the help. On some days, a student might be more successful than the teacher in getting a concept across to a classmate. Schools have reported that many students are willing to use their own free time, either during lunch or before or after school, to work with fellow students.

When working to develop a more cohesive class, it is essential to ask students about topics and activities that are important to them. Listen to the ideas students have about programs they feel are best suited for their class-room. It is always a good idea to stay informed about the mindsets of each group of students that enters your classroom. Each group has unique needs arising from societal and generational changes.

Conduct Field Studies

An excellent way to encourage students to relate is to get them out of the classroom. Packing picnic lunches, working in teams, providing community service, and riding the bus are activities that invite students to relate to each other in positive ways. Field trips can follow course material already presented in the classroom. For example, visiting a graveyard can stimulate students' imaginations and encourage creative writing. Ask a team of students to select one stone or grave marker and answer questions such as the following: "What was this person like?" "What took place in society during the person's life?" "Why did this person die?" Advanced students can even conduct actual research on the person in city library files, in old newspapers, and on the Internet. The class clown's rich imagination and quick wit enrich any field study.

A variation of a field study is a time capsule. The new year is a good time to make resolutions. Ask students to write some improvements they wish for themselves. Place the resolutions in self-addressed envelopes and seal them in a time capsule for a set period of time. At the end of the time period, open the time capsules, distribute the letters, and encourage students to talk about their improvements.

Play That Funky Music

The universal language of music should have a place in just about everything a teacher does. Music is found in every culture and has been in every culture throughout human history. It may be that humans have a cognitive developmental path for understanding music not unlike that for speech. It is known that the organizing factor in music is the beat. Without the beat (except in very rare circumstances), there is no music. Beat is the heart of music. Harmony and melody are secondary.

Samantha Duchemin, music percussionist and master teacher, maintains that drumming brings abstract concepts to students in a deeply tactile way. According to Duchemin, learning the rhythm and beat of numbers, the cadence of language, and even our own heartbeat through drumming activities makes abstract ideas come alive. Using music as a teaching tool helps reach class clowns and provides them with exciting learning experiences. As one little clown said, "When I get up and do something, I learn better."

Music and all of the other arts are not frills. They are at the heart of education. In physical education and gym classes, music adds tempo to warm-up exercises and makes workout sessions enjoyable. In history class, it is used to identify and give flavor to a particular historical event. In art class, it sets a mood for artistry. In math class, it teaches timing, synchronization, and tempo. In English class, music inspires poetry. In the school cafeteria, soft music helps make lunchtime an enjoyable event.

A clever example of using music and dance as teaching tools is provided by St. John Neumann Catholic School in Columbia, South Carolina. One year, the school's sixth graders developed a musical expedition through ancient civilizations called "DIG IT!" The students' musical traveled back 7,000 years through Mesopotamia, ancient Egypt, and the Golden Age of Greece. In one number, a group of suffering serfs built the pyramids while singing "In My Tomb." This was a delightful take on a popular song titled "In My Room."

Music is probably the most important thing, aside from themselves, their family and friends, and their humor, that class clowns care about. Obtain a radio or a CD player for students to use at the beginning of homeroom or at break times. Invite students to bring their favorite CDs to school. This adds a new and exciting dimension to school activities. It also is an easy way to find out what interests students. This finding might help you develop fresh and creative avenues for teaching the curriculum.

A fun activity is to randomly assign students to small groups and have each group select and sing a favorite television commercial, converting the words of the commercial to fit a current academic concept. Teachers can encourage students to create new endings for fables, fairy tales, and nursery rhymes and rewrite proverbs and maxims. All of these activities stimulate learning and help reduce boredom. They are also particularly useful in teaching class clowns.

WHAT CLASS CLOWNS CAN TEACH US ABOUT RELATING

Teaching can be a very lonely profession. Once the classroom doors close, teachers might not see each other for hours. For some lonely teachers, the daily routine might only include PCP (parking lot, classroom, parking lot). To make up for this isolation, teachers should take every opportunity to reach out and form relationships. Some ways to reach out include (1) savoring every moment, (2) enjoying life, and (3) fighting fair.

Savor Every Moment

Death is breathing down our necks at every turn. As Shakespeare reminds us, "Golden lads and girls all must, as chimney-sweepers, come to dust." We are alive for a brief time, so we should savor every moment. Don't get trapped by living in the past or future. Beware of a "wait until" mentality:

"Wait until summer recess, then I'll be happy."

"Wait until I finish school, then I'll be happy."

"Wait until I get married, then I'll be happy."

"Wait until I have children, then I'll be happy."

"Wait until I get that promotion, then I'll be happy."

"Wait until I retire, then I'll be happy."

"Wait until I die and go to heaven, then I'll be happy."

You will probably be as happy in the future as you are right now unless you recognize, appreciate, and savor what you have right now. An essential part of savoring is to laugh at yourself. One elementary teacher reported scolding her students by saying, "You're acting like a bunch of kids." Then she remembered she was lecturing second graders.

Claudia Cornett, a colleague and friend, recommends that teachers set up a special place to save all of the anecdotes, stories, cartoons, and jokes that make them laugh again and again. She suggests that these mementos be pulled out when the teacher needs a lift. Claudia also suggests that teachers share their "pepper-uppers" by placing them on bulletin boards, in newsletters, or in the teachers' lounge.

A dear friend and funny lady, Judy Dixon, shared an experience she had that illustrates that it's never too late for some things. She said that as a little girl she had one great dream, to become a ballerina. Her bedroom walls were covered with photographs of ballerinas she had lovingly cut from magazines. But genes pulled a trick. Judy kept growing. By fourth grade, she was almost as tall as her teacher.

At this point, the unintentional killers of the dream stepped in. "Darling, Sweetheart, Angel," they said, "there are lots of things you can be in this world, but not a ballerina. Ballerinas must be tiny figurines, and you're a long-stemmed American rose. You can never be a ballerina." Reluctantly, Judy took her photos off the wall, one by one. But she did not completely abandon her dream. She grew up, became an elementary school teacher, married, and had a family.

One day, at the age of thirty-eight, Judy was having Sunday dinner with her husband and three teenage daughters. Suddenly, right in the middle of a bite of food, she heard the big "click." The lightbulb came on in her head. She placed her fork on her plate, looked calmly at her family, and said, "I am going to take ballet lessons."

Her husband, totally surprised, said, "Oh no, you're not."

Judy responded, "Oh yes, I am."

Her three daughters, in their high-pitched, dental-drill voices, said in unison, "Oh no, you're not." And Judy replied, "Oh yes, I am."

The next day, Judy went to school all excited. A faculty meeting was scheduled after school, and the principal always started each meeting with five minutes of happy talk. He believed that no one could teach on an empty spirit. At the faculty meeting, the principal asked faculty members for happy comments. Judy stood and announced, "I am going to take ballet lessons."

And all of her colleagues said in unison, "Oh no, you're not."

Judy responded, "Oh yes, I am."

After the faculty meeting ended, Judy headed for the local dance studio. She approached the ballet master and explained, "I want to take ballet lessons." And to his eternal credit, the ballet master said, "Come on in. However, I don't think we have a tutu that would fit you." "Fine," Judy responded. "We'll sew two tutus together and call them four by fours."

Judy began her lessons. Week after week, month after month, she went to the dance studio to live her dream. Then came the gut check—the dance recital.

And her husband said, "Oh no, you're not!"

And her three daughters said, "Oh no, you're not!"

And all of her school colleagues said, "Oh no, you're not!"

And Judy said, "Oh yes, I am!"

During the next few days Judy practiced diligently to prepare herself for the recital.

The recital was held in a rented auditorium, and all the proud parents were there. The program began with the tiny tot beginners and continued with the intermediates, the seniors, and the advanced. When all had danced, the house lights grew dim, the spotlight came on, and out of the wings came a thirty-eight-year-old elementary school teacher. Judy danced like there was nobody watching and loved like she'd never be hurt. Later, Judy told me that she was the only dancer during the entire program to receive a standing ovation.

The message is clear: In a world that is continually telling us what we cannot do, it takes a great deal of assertiveness to reach out and savor every moment of what life offers. Those who have the courage to dance will always find a melody.

Enjoy Life

There are a million ways for teachers to enjoy life. Have you noticed that when you are having fun and laughing, other people are drawn in? They want to have fun, too. In some strange way, many people need permission to have fun. Class clowns give permission to others by who they are as much as what they do.

There appear to be four kinds of people in this world: sad, mad, scared, and cheerful. Each represents a particular outlook on life.

Sad people believe there is no party. Life is a vale of tears. Sad people are those who, when they smell flowers, look around for a funeral. They have a flair for transmitting messages of hopelessness and despair.

Mad people believe there is a party, but they're not invited. Few things are as disturbing to them as passing a friend's house and seeing a line of parked cars.

Pleasures being enjoyed by others—and appearing to be denied them—can be maddening.

Scared people believe that there is a party, they are invited, but they are not going. For them, life is filled with anxiety and terror. They live a rigid, fearful, and encapsulated existence.

Finally, there are the cheerful people. They believe there's a party and they're giving it. They embrace Ben Franklin's advice: "If you would have guests merry with cheer, be so yourself, or so at least appear." Cheerful people not only inspirit themselves, but they also are a beneficial presence in the lives of others. The class clowns' witty comments invite others to be witty.

I wrote a short vignette to illustrate the power of living life fully. The following story is about a man who absolutely craves salami:

The man walks into a room, and there is the most beautiful salami in the world, the mother of all salamis. He dashes across the room and prepares to take a big bite, when a thunderous voice booms, "YOU CANNOT HAVE THE SALAMI!"

The man looks around, sees no one, but says, "OK, I'll just take half of the salami."

The booming voice replies, "YOU CANNOT HAVE HALF OF THE SALAMI!"

So the man says, "Well, I'll just take the very end of the salami."

The voice responds, "YOU CANNOT HAVE THE END EITHER!"

And the man replies, "I'll just stand here and look at this beautiful salami."

The powerful voice says, "YOU CAN'T LOOK AT THE SALAMI!"

To which the man says, "OK, I'll close my eyes and just touch the salami."

The voice shouts, "YOU CANNOT TOUCH THE SALAMI!"

The man responds, "I'll put my hands behind my back and just smell the salami."

And the voice warns, "YOU CANNOT SMELL THE SALAMI EITHER!"

Then the man responds, "Let's you and me just talk about the salami."

And the voice booms out, "WE WILL NOT TALK ABOUT THE SALAMI!"

So the man says, "I'll go home and dream about the salami, and you can't stop me."

The point of my salami story is to remind us that just because we can't have everything we want, and do everything we want to do, we can always have something and do something to live a more cheerful life. Here is how William Saroyan, in the play *The Time of Your Life* (Potter, 1948), encouraged us to live a cheerful existence:

In the time of your life, live—so that in that good time there shall be no ugliness or death for yourself or for any life your life touches. See goodness everywhere, and when it is found, bring it out of its hiding-place and let it be free and unashamed. . . . In the time of your life, live—so that in that wondrous time you shall not add to the misery and sorrow of the world, but shall smile to the infinite delight and mystery of it. (p. 58)

As evidenced throughout this book, while class clowns may not know happiness, they are alive and full of good cheer. They advise us to be aware of and savor every minute of our lives. How easy it is to overlook life's joys. Give more attention to life's small pleasures and wonders. Think about the smell of a flower bud, the sound of a mockingbird, the sight of a dear friend, the taste of a fresh peach, or the feel of a cool breeze on a hot day. Class clowns remind us that we are alive. As one class clown commented in a written essay, "Dead noses smell no roses."

Fight Fair

Class clowns are not afraid to fight for their own rights. Friendly clowns fight fair by recognizing and respecting human decency. They also respect the rights of others. Being human, we are tempted to run rough-shod over people, particularly when we have the wit and desire to do so. We have all known hostile clowns who achieve a certain kind of humor through hurtful practices. However, in the final analysis, hostile clowns usually pay a high price for denying the rights of others and ignoring their feelings.

Don't be a dirty fighter. Fighting fair means being courageous in difficult times, courteous to everyone, chivalrous toward weaker individuals, and considerate of the defeated. It also means winning and losing gracefully. Humor that demeans, humiliates, or denies the rights of others is to be avoided, even if this hostile humor is funny and produces laughter.

I speak before audiences several dozen times a year. During my talks, I am tempted to use material that is guaranteed to get a big laugh from ninety-five percent of the audience. However, the humor may be offensive to the remaining five percent. For this reason, I never use the material. This is not because of my concerns about political correctness. It is because I seek to fight fair by respecting the feelings of fellow human beings, particularly those in the minority.

There are times when the desire to "kick pomposity in the ass," as Charles Chaplin noted, is overwhelming. An example is an exchange of messages between Cornelius Vanderbilt and George Westinghouse in 1872. Westinghouse contacted Vanderbilt and asked him to listen to his idea for inventing an air brake. The crusty old president of the New York Central Railroad replied, "I have no time to waste on fools." Later, after the Pennsylvania Railroad successfully tested the brake, Vanderbilt summoned Westinghouse to see him. The inventor replied, "I have no time to waste on fools." In rare instances, hostile humor is understandable and even justifiable.

Fighting fair means keeping the door open for conciliation. Sometimes, conflict is inevitable, but after the battle is over it is important to restore a noncombative relationship. Simply solving a conflict may be insufficient. The crucial part in conflict management is restoring relationships that have been damaged by the situation. If not addressed, the situation can extend far beyond the original conflict.

Breaking clean means no hard feelings. An important part of fair fighting it to learn to forgive. What is done is done, so let it be. For example, if a student must be removed from the classroom, or suspended for misbehavior, when the student returns to class the slate should be clean. There is a proverb that the person who seeks revenge should dig two graves. Remember to forget, forget to remember. Buddy Hackett, the wonderful rubber-faced comedian with the heavy Brooklyn accent said, "I never hold a grudge because while I'm being angry the other guy is out dancing." Holding on to resentment and anger, and dwelling on revenge, are self-defeating. Clowns remind us to play the music and win and lose gracefully.

There is one additional factor in fighting fair: seek to avoid battles before they start. There is great value in sensing difficult situations before they occur. Sensing the approach of problems is a special talent of class clowns. Phil Silvers (1973), a classic comedian, describes how comedians sense problems:

> The road requires an extra talent—survival. Experienced troupers acquire the art of sniffing out catastrophe before it happens. You have to be able to change direction, improvise instantly. On tour, only one thing is certain. If it is impossible for the conductor to fall into the orchestra pit and break his leg, he will do it. (p. 188)

Fighting fair through the use of humor is a wonderful investment. Humor is a great weapon of power, but it must be used appropriately, caringly, and decently. Human relationships are vital in living life fully.

This chapter focused on the class clown's signature tendency to relate. It stressed the importance of creating and maintaining an inviting classroom. The classroom is like a big bowl of gelatin—touch it anywhere and the whole thing jiggles. Understanding the gelatin principle helps us to remember that everything—temperature, time of day, color of walls, tone of voice—adds to or subtracts from a bright and welcoming classroom. Any effort to make the classroom more inviting positively affects the behavior of class clowns.

In addition to offering advice on how to teach class clowns, this chapter provided some suggestions from class clowns on how teachers can savor every moment, enjoy life, and fight fair. Chapter 6 concludes the book by describing how clowns cope with expectations and what they can teach us about coping.

ENCORE

(A REAPPEARANCE AND ADDITIONAL PERFORMANCE)

1. Value Esthetics. In Japan, the tea ceremony enriches all of the senses. For the eyes are flower arrangements; for the nose, the rich small of tea; for the ears, the sound of hot water being poured; for the mouth, the taste of the tea; and for the hands and feet, the correctness of form. Do what you can to enrich your classroom by using all of your senses.

Suggestion: Seek help to make over the faculty lounge/workroom. Fresh paint, area rugs, good lighting, fresh air, and comfortable furniture can work wonders. When the lounge is newly decorated, arrange for refreshments and send an invitation to all faculty and staff to attend the "Grand Opening."

2. Sharpen Your Image. When you go to school, dress like you're going somewhere important. Take a good look in the mirror to ensure that you are reasonably well groomed. Dressing well suggests authority. It improves student discipline as well as school safety.

Suggestion: Go through your wardrobe and give to charity everything you don't like or have not worn in years (the clothing that "shrunk" in the closet). Then buy a few new items. Your new clothes will be noticed by others and will add to your self-confidence.

3. Conquer Haste. Sometimes emotions can get out of hand. A good way to calm down is to listen carefully, take your time, lower your voice, and speak slowly.

Suggestion: In a private conference, allow others to climb "Emotion Mountain"—without interruption. If you block their climb (to express themselves), you only make things worse. Allowing others to express their feelings slows things down and may result in a compromise.

Coping

I've always felt like there might be a different way to look at things. I've always tried to make that the essence of my work—my comedy work—simply because I always think it's important for people to have two or three different ways to look at stuff, not that they have to agree, and I'm not necessarily out to change anybody's mind. It's just the way that I am.

—Whoopi Goldberg in
Comedians (Grace, 1991, p. 42)

*C*oping is the fourth and final signature tendency of class clowns. Coping is the ability to learn from experience, to take advantage of situations, and to deal successfully with life's demands. The great comedian W. C. Fields believed in taking advantage of whatever windfalls the Lord provided. When he was spotted reading the Bible, he replied that he was looking for loopholes.

THE VALUE OF COPING

Willie Cosh, my Scottish friend, shared a story of an attempt by a class clown to outsmart the national English examination. The clown had gambled that a fantasy news story would be assigned as the essay topic. (Fantasy assignments had often appeared in previous exams.) Therefore, he prepared an essay about the discovery of a new animal in Kenya. Unfortunately, the assigned topic was to write an essay on the prompt "The best dream I ever had." The clown's solution was to write a few paragraphs and then write, "We interrupt this young boy's dream to bring you fantastic news from Africa." He then wrote his essay of choice and passed the exam.

Class clowns are often able to turn painful things upside down. A weakness becomes a strength. By surrendering, the class clown becomes powerful. The wonderful comedian Woody Allen described the process of coping. He explained that he always carried a cutlass with him. By doing so, he could take care of himself in case of danger. If an emergency were to arise, he could press the cutlass handle, and it would turn into a cane, which would bring him sympathy.

Judy Engel, retired math teacher from the Bronx High School of Science in New York, shared a story about one class clown who was often "out of line." The math teacher's favorite penalty for student misbehavior was to require the erring student to write the multiplication table. Knowing the penalty for misconduct, the clown wrote the multiplication table in advance in preparation of the punishment sure to come. Developing strategies for handling stressful situations and hardships is essential in coping with life's tribulations.

How to Teach Class Clowns Through Coping

In spite of tribulations, class clowns find ways to face the demands of life. One way or another, they are able to cope with the expectations of school and society, although often with a certain fine madness. When a teacher asked a first-grade clown what comes after the letter *A* in the alphabet, he answered, "All of them."

Many clowns learn to cope with the expectations of school personnel by using their sharp sense of humor. One junior high school clown arrived late for class. When the teacher reprimanded him for his tardiness, he replied, "I'll make up for it. I'll leave early."

Here are some coping techniques that teachers can put to good use in working with class clowns.

Keep the Volcano From Erupting

Look around the classroom and observe student activity and energy levels. What is in the air? Is something special needed to get students focused on class material? Monitor the mood and energy level of students. Determine the best thing to do at this moment to get students involved in learning. If students are fidgety, restless, or bored, it is a good idea to take a few minutes for stretch exercises. Ask everyone to stand and do a few simple exercises. "Simon Says" is an excellent game to wake everybody up.

The cardinal sin of teaching is to bore students to death. Consider boredom the number one enemy in the classroom. Devise puzzles, games, contests, exercises, demonstrations, presentations, competitions, and challenges to fight boredom. Ask students to rewrite proverbs; develop new lyrics to old, familiar songs; or create new endings to well-known stories. And remember this truth: "If you are bored as a teacher, it's probably because you are boring."

One simple way to avoid boredom is to maintain a giveaway library. Teachers can keep a fresh stock of books on hand by visiting garage and yard sales, flea markets, and thrift stores. It's worth the small cost of a used book for a class clown to hear a teacher say, "Here is a book I want you to have and enjoy. I think it was written just for you."

The old adage "the devil has work for idle hands" carries a special message for teachers who work with class clowns. Successful teachers of class clowns consider good classroom behavior as a logical result of their ability to involve students actively in their education. These teachers understand that silence, stillness, and boredom require inordinate amounts of time and energy to "control" students.

A primary requirement in teaching class clowns is to keep them busy so that they don't have time to be disruptive. Giving all students clear responsibilities via a job chart (distributing and collecting material, arranging the classroom furniture, setting up or taking down audiovisual equipment, tidying up, presenting reports) keeps class clowns busy and involved. Class activities should be, as much as possible, activity based.

One successful way to change the pace in classroom routines (which can be deadly boring) is to assign two-minute seminars. Randomly assign each student a partner (teachers should make the assignments to avoid cliques). Ask each pair to create a response to a question posed by you. After about two minutes, ask the partners to report their response. If students know in advance that they will be called on to present their work before the entire class, they are more likely to stay on task. These activities require a lot of teacher preparation, but they pay off in good student conduct.

One teacher explained how she kept one class clown busy and involved. She assigned the class clown two desks. Whenever the clown felt bored, he had permission to quietly change desks.

Listen to the Ice

The fox in Aesop's fable avoided falling through the ice by carefully listening to its sound. Successful teachers solve discipline problems before they happen by such means as moving toward the source of misbehavior, lowering their voice, calling on a student, or shifting to a more interesting part of the lesson. Successful teachers are also able to meet the needs of individual students while continuing small-group activities. The secret is to maintain good eye contact with both the individual student and the rest of the class. One teacher referred to this talent as developing "linebacker's eyes."

A way to avoid falling through the ice is to assign insight cards turned in by students at regular weekly intervals. These insight cards, created from regular index cards, are designed to open dialogue between the teacher and the students. The cards provide a regular vehicle for students to voice concerns, offer suggestions, share observations, and express vigorous dissent. Class clowns prize insight cards because the cards encourage classroom dialogue.

Follow the Six C's

One of the marvels of steel is that it can bend without breaking. Smart teachers remain flexible under stress. Both class clowns and teachers can benefit by using the six C's to manage troublesome situations. The trick is to start with the lowest possible C, "Concern," and move to the next higher C only as absolutely necessary:

Concern	The situation is significant enough to require attention.
Confer	Politely explain the concern to the other party in private.
Consult	Remind the other party of logical consequences.
Confront	Give a serious warning of possible penalties.
Combat	Administer a reasonable and enforceable penalty.
Conciliate	Attempt to bury the hatchet and rebuild relationships.

By intentionally following the six C's, and striving to manage conflicts at the lowest possible level, teachers and students will save energy, reduce hostility, avoid acrimony, and successfully manage many disputes.

WHAT CLASS CLOWNS CAN TEACH US ABOUT COPING

Teaching is a personal and delicate relationship among and between human beings. Coping with this relationship is a major challenge for teachers. The following suggestions are based on a class clown attitude toward life.

Capitalize on Bad Moments

Class clowns tend to handle bad moments better than most people. They understand that, sooner or later, the worst events are bound to occur. Clowns remind us that a good response to difficult moments is to get the laughter going. From a class clown's perspective, it is both sad and hilarious when something cannot be handled, controlled, or even understood. Here is an example.

When my grandson, Jason, was about nine years old, he and I traveled together on a flight from Omaha, Nebraska, to Greensboro, North Carolina. During the flight, he became deathly airsick and gagged or threw up through much of the trip. When we landed at the Greensboro airport, we walked down the concourse. Jason's face was as green as grass, and he was clutching his barf bag. As we passed a hot dog stand, Jason looked up and said in a shaky voice, "Granddaddy, can I have a hot dog?" Although I was concerned that Jason was so sick, I thought his question was hilarious.

When you're facing a bad situation and everything seems to be going against you, hang in there. It may be that at that moment your luck will change. The gods favor the warrior who has a sense of humor. Here is how Joey Bishop, a professional comedian, described how he used humor to survive: "If I was going to fight with a guy, if it came to a fistfight, if I could get myself out of it with humor, I did. There's no question the guy could knock my brains out. I would say, 'I just want to warn you, if I hit you, I'm gonna' go down'" (Wilde, 1968, p. 125). Capitalizing on bad moments by talking one's way out of trouble is a hallmark of class clowns.

In my own life as a class clown, if I were late to class, I could usually talk myself out of trouble by inventing outrageous stories that included kidnappings, raging elephants, terrorists, drunken monkeys, and encounters of the worst kind. If I could elicit a smile from the teacher, I knew I was home safe.

It was probably a class clown, masquerading as an actor, who took to the stage in the role of Shakespeare's Hamlet. When the audience began to throw tomatoes and boo him off the stage, he stopped his soliloquy in midsentence and said to the audience, "Take it easy fellows. I didn't write this crap."

Count on Serendipity

Clowns handle bad moments by taking advantage of serendipity. Basically, serendipity enables a person who is searching for one thing to accidentally find something entirely different. Many of the world's great discoveries have been the result of serendipity. The scientific world would be a great deal poorer without the effects of serendipity.

The word "serendipity" comes from a Persian folktale describing the antics of the three princes of Serendip. Although they were blessed with shrewdness, they also relied on chance. A sample of serendipity may be found in the early Hollywood film *Queen Christina*. John Gilbert discovers that his male roommate is actually a beautiful woman. In a masterful understatement, he comments, "Life is so gloriously improbable."

Clowns rely on both luck and shrewdness. They tend to have a sense of the funny thing to do under a certain set of circumstances. It is only later that logic comes into play. The professional comedian Tim Conway provides a good example of handling bad moments. Tim's elementary teacher asked him who was the twenty-fourth president of the United States. Not knowing the answer, Tim responded, "Well, it wasn't anybody in my family."

Find Humor in Frustrations

Capitalizing on frustrations means to seek and discover the humor that is almost always embedded in them. According to the great humorist James Thurber, humor is emotional chaos remembered in tranquility. Here is a story of total frustration, remembered with laughter, from my own life.

Several years ago, I gave a talk at Brock University in St. Catharines, Ontario, Canada. After my presentation, I returned to the Toronto airport, where I was to proceed to my home in Greensboro, North Carolina. There were no direct flights from Toronto to Greensboro, so it was necessary to fly into the New York airport and then connect with a flight home.

At the New York airport, I inadvertently boarded the wrong airplane. Instead of going to Greensboro, North Carolina, I was on my way to Greenville, South Carolina. As we landed, the flight attendant welcomed us to Greenville. I listened to her, then thought to myself, "Why can't this airline get its act together? The flight attendant doesn't even know where she is." Then I looked out the window and saw a large neon sign reading "Welcome to Greenville." Only then did realize my blunder.

As soon as the exit doors opened, I hurried off the plane, ran up to the nearest airline agent, and explained that I had gotten on the wrong airplane. He apologized and said that the airline gate agents were supposed to check boarding passes. Somehow, I had slipped by. The agent arranged to reroute me on another flight that he thought stopped in Atlanta. There I could catch a connecting flight home. To make up for my inconvenience, he upgraded my ticket to first class.

Just before the doors closed on my departure flight from Greenville, two women entered the plane. They settled in their first-class seats directly across the aisle from me. They were a rather odd couple. One of the women was over six feet tall, and the other was only three feet tall. I studied them out of the corner of my eye. I could not figure out who they were or why they were in my first-class section (you can get used to wealth very quickly).

Finally, my curiosity got the better of me. I leaned over and spoke to the tall lady across the aisle, "You're flight attendants, being rerouted somewhere, aren't you?" (I knew that they were not flight attendants.) The tall lady responded, "No, we're not flight attendants, but if I tell you who we are, you must promise that you will never tell anyone as long as you live." I promised, Boy Scout's honor (which gives you some insight into my character). The tall lady pointed to the short one next to her and asked me, "Do you know who this is?" I responded that I had no idea. She said, "You should know. You've seen her many times." I protested that I had never seen the lady in my life. The tall lady laughed and said, "Oh yes, you have. We are from Disney World, and this is Minnie Mouse. I am the Disney representative. This little lady next to me dons a costume to play the role of Minnie. Today we led a parade in Greenville, South Carolina. Now we're on this nonstop flight to *Dallas, Texas.*"

I turned and looked out my porthole into the darkness. I thought, "How appropriate. Here is Minnie Mouse to the right, and Goofy (myself) to the left, flying off to Dallas in the middle of the night." It did not seem humorous at the time, but looking back it was a very funny experience.

Making the best of bad situations is a hallmark of humor. For example, a professional comedian was known along Broadway in New York as a great dresser. His suits were handmade and of the finest fabrics. Unfortunately, he never paid his tailor. One of the tailor's friends suggested that the comedian was a total deadbeat. "The bum probably doesn't have a penny to his name." The tailor answered, "He must have money. Look at the way he dresses!"

Whoopi Goldberg, the loveable comedienne, described how to capitalize on bad moments this way, "You always have to keep in mind that you're going to have good days and bad days and not all materials work for all audiences." Class clowns accept the reality of bad situations, but they capitalize on them by being of good cheer and growing personally from the experience. To laugh at troubles, if they are unavoidable, is an important lesson we can learn from class clowns.

Be Suspicious of Hearsay

We know ourselves primarily from hearsay. From birth onward, we are enclosed in a particular world. We spend every moment in this world. This world protects and enhances us, or it debases and abandons us. Richard Lewis, standup comedian, said, "People become unnecessarily neurotic because they unthinkingly accept other people's perceptions of who they are. I, for one, for years always felt defined by other people. So basically, when I go on stage, I say, 'I'm not crazy, they're crazy'" (Grace, 1991, p. 106).

I have a personal story that illustrates why we should not take ourselves too seriously. When I was a little boy, growing up in a small Virginia town, few joys surpassed going barefoot. I recall one summer day, as I was standing in my grandparents' front yard, barefooted, some bigger boys came wandering by. As they passed me, one boy happened to glance down and said, "Hey, everybody, look here. Look at Purkey's second toe. He's got turkey toes!" The other boys walked over, looked at my long second toes, and agreed, "Yep, he's got turkey toes all right." I stared down at my bare feet, and for the first time I noticed my second toes. I have long second toes that stretch far beyond all the others.

"Turkey Toe Purkey," the boys chanted. They soon tired of teasing me and headed for a nearby pond to throw rocks at frogs. As the gunslinger Paladin said in the television series *Have Gun, Will Travel,* "Small boys throw rocks at frogs in fun, but frogs die in earnest." From that day on, I dared not go barefoot. I didn't want anyone to discover the terrible dark secret of my long second toes. I was the only kid in the swimming pool wearing sneakers.

I carried the deep, dark secret of the long second toes with me until I was a high school senior. In those days (back when the earth was cooling), it was a yearly ritual to load all of the seniors in school buses and take them on a three-day senior-class trip to Washington, DC.

The first day we visited the United States Mint. The second day was reserved for the Smithsonian. On the third day, we visited the United States Capitol building.

We scampered off the school bus, climbed the marble steps, and entered the Capitol. On entering the Rotunda, I noticed that there were many life-size marble statues of presidents and other famous people. As I wandered around the Rotunda, I stopped before the statue of George Washington. For some strange reason, George was dressed in a Roman toga. He was wearing sandals, open-toed sandals. I happened to look down and there they were! The longest second toes I had even seen. They went off the pedestal and down the side.

I stared at George Washington's turkey toes while saying to myself, "All these years I have been paying interest on a bill that I never owed." It was at that moment that I learned not to take myself too seriously. This is especially true when it comes to talking to ourselves about ourselves. In an earlier book, I called this private conversation the whispering self (Purkey, 2000).

The knowledge we gradually develop about ourselves and the world is organized into internal dialogue. This self-talk is what we say privately to ourselves about our selves and what we listen to in our heads. It is this whispering self that either summons us to be cheerful, optimistic, and hopeful or to be sad, pessimistic, and hopeless.

Class clowns are more likely than nonclowns to have a positive, optimistic approach to life. This approach is evidenced by Clarence Day (1993), in his book *Life with Father*, when he discusses his father's plan to purchase a new plot in the cemetery, a plot all to himself. His father claimed he would buy a corner lot, so he could get out. Father's upbeat attitude serves as a valuable model for living a cheerful life.

With pessimists, the whispering self discourages feelings of confidence and efficacy. A negative whispering self informs us that things are more difficult than they really are. It reminds us that we lack the ability to understand or solve problems. This negative voice speaks of fear, anxiety, and defeat. It is difficult to achieve much of anything while listening to an inner voice filled with pessimism, self-doubt, and even self-hatred. Imagine an inner voice that lacks confidence in oneself:

Noninvesting "I'm afraid to try new things."

Nonasserting "I have a hard time speaking out."

Nonrelating   "I never know what to say to people."

Noncoping   "I've never been any good at math."

Compare those negative comments with those of a positive whispering self:

Investing "I like to volunteer for things."

Asserting "I make time for what I want to do."

Relating   "I work well with others."

Coping   "I can do lots of things well."

Often we tell ourselves that we cannot invest, assert, relate, or cope, even when such things are not true. The lack of positive and realistic self-talk establishes limits to performance, and these limits are as "real" as this book.

A delightful tribute to upbeat thinking is offered in the unforgettable stories of *Winnie-the-Pooh,* written by A. A. Milne (1926). Eeyore, the old gray donkey, is always fixated on what is wrong with situations. When he loses his tail, he says, "Someone must have taken it . . . how like them." To which Pooh responds, "I, Winnie-the Pooh, will find your tail for you." Winnie-the-Pooh, in his many escapades, was clearly a class clown.

Class clowns are largely successful in coping with life's demands. They make the most of challenging situations.

Seeking a cheerful life can be summed up with a little poem I wrote:

If I can't be a forest, I'll be a tree.

If I can't be an ocean, I'll be a sea.

If I can't be a lock, I'll be a key.

If I want to be cheerful, it's up to me.

CONCLUSION

And now it is time to conclude this book. Perhaps *Teaching Class Clowns* will be of service in identifying fresh ways to teach a very special, valuable, and often lovable group of students. Perhaps, too, this book will invite a greater cheerfulness, if not happiness, into your life. You are cordially summoned to invest by living to enjoy, to assert by starting to finish, to relate by giving as much as you get, and to cope by learning to survive in a challenging and threatening world.

On behalf of class clowns everywhere, young and old, I summon you most cordially to be of good cheer. Cheerfulness is a precious commodity in a world of drabness, cynicism, and despair. Cheerfulness provides a special magic that contributes to lightheartedness. Franklin D. Roosevelt (n.d.) paid tribute to those who bring a special gift to our fellow beings with these words:

> I doubt if there is among us a more useful citizen
> Than the one who holds the secret of banishing gloom,
> Of making tears give way to laughter,
> Of supplanting desolation and despair
> With hope and courage,
> For hope and courage always go with a light heart.

Treasure class clowns, for they inspirit us all.

A FINAL ENCORE

(A REAPPEARANCE AND ADDITIONAL PERFORMANCE)

1. Think More and Act Less. According to Zen martial artists (Hyams, 1982; Tsunetomo, 1983), to lose your temper is to lose yourself. It is hard to imagine teachers controlling class clowns without first controlling themselves. When you act in anger, you allow others to control you.

Suggestion: Push from behind rather than resisting from the front. For example, listen to an angry person without interruption. After you have listened carefully, say, "Let me see if I have this correctly," then repeat back to the angry person what he or she said. This shows you've been listening and that you understand the person's concern. It also allows you to interrupt without being rude.

2. Know Your Limits. Be willing to correct yourself when you make a mistake. When teachers try to cover up their errors, it becomes uncomfortable for everyone.

Suggestion: Quickly own up to mistakes. By correcting yourself immediately, the mistakes usually disappear. Trying to stonewall an error only makes you look like a phony or worse. Many celebrities and politicians have suffered disaster, not because of bad conduct but because they attempted to cover up their misbehavior with distortions and lies.

3. Be a Self-Righting Doll. Remember the rubberized blow-up doll that was a self-righting punching bag? It had a weighted bottom that allowed it to bounce back up no matter how hard it was hit. Humor is a great bounce-back defense during embarrassing predicaments. Difficult situations can be neutralized if teachers can see the humor in embarrassing moments.

Suggestion: A great way to bounce back is to laugh at ourselves. Laughter can lower tensions and give everyone a breather. It also provides stress relief and facilitates healing. The goal is to have everyone laugh with you, not at you.

> And had the luck, with much ado
>
> To live a fool, and yet die wise.
>
> —Cervantes (1950)

Bibliography

Allen, S. (1968). *The funny men.* New York: Simon & Schuster.

Allen, S. (1982). *More funny people.* New York: Stein and Day.

Bacon, J. (1976). *Hollywood is a four letter word.* New York: Avon Books.

Bacon, J. (1985). *How sweet it is: The Jackie Gleason story.* New York: St. Martin's Press.

Bandura, A. (1994). *Self-efficacy.* In V. S. Ramachaudram (Ed.), *Encyclopedia of human behavior* (Vol. 4, pp. 71–81). New York: Academic Press.

Berle, M. (1989). *Milton Berle's private joke file.* New York: Crown.

Burns, G. (1976). *George Burns living it up, or they still love me in Altoona.* New York: G. P. Putnam.

Butzin, S. M. (2005). *Joyful classrooms in an age of accountability.* Bloomington, IN: Phi Delta Kappa International.

Byrd, T. (1982). *Letters to Carl.* Austin, TX: T. Byrd Roadrunner Press.

Cervantes, Miguel, de. (1950). *The adventures of Don Quixote.* Baltimore: Penguin Books.

Cohen, J. (1970). *The essential Lenny Bruce.* New York: Douglas Books.

Cornett, C. (2001). *Learning through laughter—Again.* Bloomington, IN: Phi Delta Kappa Educational Foundation.

Damico, S. B., & Purkey, W. W. (1979). Class clowns: A study of middle school students. *American Educational Research Journal, 15,* 3.

Day, C. (1993). *Life with father.* Pleasantville, NY: Reader's Digest.

Frank, L. R. (2000). *Random House Webster's wit and humor quotationary.* New York: Random House.

Gardner, H. (1962). *A thousand clowns: A new comedy.* New York: Random House.

Gardner, H. (1999). *Intelligence reframed: Multiple intelligences for the 21st century.* New York: Basic Books.

Gladwell, M. (2000). *The tipping point: How little things can make a big difference.* New York: Little, Brown.

Gladwell, M. (2004). *Blink: The power of thinking without thinking.* New York: Little, Brown.

Gorham, J., & Christophel, G. (1990). The relationship of teachers' use of humor in the classroom to students' learning. *Communication Education, 39*(19), 46–62.

Grace, A. (1991). *Comedians.* Charlottesville, VA: Professional Photography Division, Eastman Kodak.

Gregory, D. (1964). *Nigger.* New York: Simon & Schuster.

Handey, J. (1992). *Deep thoughts.* New York: Berkley Books.

Harper, K. L. (1991). *Inferred and professed self-concepts of gifted and average middle school students.* Unpublished doctoral dissertation, University of North Carolina at Greensboro.

Harper, K. L., & Purkey, W. W. (1993). Self-concept-as-learner of middle level students. *Research in Middle Level Education, 17*(1), 79–89.

Hyams, J. (1982). *Zen in the martial arts.* New York: Bantam Books.

Johnson, G. W. (1934). *A little night music.* New York: Harper & Brothers.

Johnston, L. (1994). *For better or for worse: It's the thought that counts.* Kansas City, MO: Andrews & McMeel.

Kesey, K. (1962). *One flew over the cuckoo's nest.* New York: Viking.

Klein, R. (2005). *The amorous busboy of Decatur Avenue: A memoir.* New York: Touchstone Books.

Leno, J. (with Bill Zehme). (1996). *Leading with my chin.* New York: HarperCollins.

Madigan, C. O., & Elwood, A. (1998). *When they were kids: Over 400 sketches of famous childhoods.* New York: Random House.

Mamoulian, R. (Director). (1933). *Queen Christina* [Motion picture]. United States: Warner Brothers.

McCabe, J. (1985). *Mr. Laurel and Mr. Hardy: An affectionate biography.* New York: Doubleday. (Original work published 1961)

Meadows, A. (1994). *Audrey Meadows: Love, Alice.* New York: Crown.

Milne, A. A. (1926). *Winnie-the-Pooh.* New York: E. P. Dutton.

Moore, A. S. (2005, July 31). How to identify a gifted child. *New York Times,* p. A10.

Nachman, G. (2003). *Seriously funny: The rebel comedians of the 1950s and 1960s.* New York: Pantheon Books.

Nilsen, A. P., & Nilsen, D. L. F. (2000). *Encyclopedia of 20th-century American humor.* Westport, CT: Greenwood.

Patinkin, S. (2000). *The second city: Backstage at the world's greatest comedy theater.* Naperville, IL: Sourcebooks.

Potter, H. C. (Director). (1948). *The time of your life* [Motion picture]. United States: United Artists.

Purkey, W. W. (1970). *Self-concept and school achievement.* Englewood Cliffs, NJ: Prentice Hall.

Purkey, W. W. (1973). Miracle at Herbert Hoover High. *Alpha Delta Kappan, 3,* 2.

Purkey, W. W. (2000). *What students say to themselves: Internal dialogue and school success.* Thousand Oaks, CA: Corwin.

Purkey, W. W., & Novak, J. (1996). *Inviting school success: A self-concept approach to teaching, learning, and democratic practice* (3rd ed.). New York: Wadsworth.

Purkey, W. W., & Siegel, B. F. (2003). *Becoming an invitational leader.* Atlanta, GA: Humanics Press.

Roosevelt, F. D. (n.d.). *An emissary of sensitivity.* Retrieved November 4, 2005, from http://209.87.142.42/y/m/m75.htm

Russell, D. (2003). *The chalkdust trail: Memories of a pedagogue.* St. Simon, GA: D. Russell.

Saint-Exupéry, A., de. (1943). *The little prince.* New York: Harcourt, Brace.

Seligman, M. (2002). *Authentic happiness.* New York: Free Press.

Silvers, P. H. (with Robert Saffron). (1973). *This laugh is on me: The Phil Silvers' story.* Englewood Cliffs, NJ: Prentice Hall.

Snider, B. (2005, September). Clowning around. *Edutopia.* Retrieved October 20, 2005, from http://www.edutopia.org/magazine/sep_05.php

Sullivan, G. (2001). *Quotable Hollywood: The lowdown from America's film capital.* New York: Barnes & Noble Books.

Swindell, C. C. (1983). *Growing strong in the seasons of life.* Portland, OR: Multnomah Press.

Taylor, R. L. (1967). *WC Fields: His follies and fortunes.* New York: New American Library.

Tsunetomo, Y. (1983). *The book of the samurai* (W. S. Wilson, Trans.). New York: Kodansha America.

Wilde, L. (1968). *The great comedians talk about comedy.* New York: Citadel Press.

Wilde, L. (1976). *How the great comedy writers create laughter.* Chicago: Nelson-Hall.

Wilk, M. (1973). *The wit and wisdom of Hollywood.* New York: Warner.

Willis, M. (1997). *An investigation of second and third graders' oral responses to humorous children's literature.* Unpublished doctoral dissertation, University of Kentucky.

Index